# America

## A NEW ECONOMIC REALITY

*By*

### EUGENE ALBERT FISCHER

and

### ALBERT EUGENE PARISH

*Illustrations by*

### JESSE KRIMES

*Inmates of the*

### US PRISON SYSTEM

*America: A New Economic Reality*
By Eugene Albert Fischer
and Albert Eugene Parish

Illustrations by Jesse Krimes
Inmates of the US Prison System

ISBN: 1467920967
ISBN 13: 9781467920964

# Table of Contents

# Foreward

The decision to write this book grew out of our concern about the direction our country is taking economically and its resulting place in a global economy. The purpose of this book is to lay out our economic issues as we see them and offer some possible solutions. While politics is inseparable from macroeconomic policy decisions, this is not a political book per se. We offer solutions that could be described as conservative, liberal, or independent. We do not pretend to decide which solution is best but offer various solutions to those problems.

This book is not written for economists! It is written for the average American with an interest in our economic situation. We do not expect even a majority of readers to agree with all we have to say. Indeed, if a majority were to agree with any one economist this would probably signal the end of the world! We do hope that this book provokes thought among its readers, including policymakers and politicians, should they read it. We would be delighted to hear from any readers, especially average citizens, who are most affected by our problems and some of our suggested solutions.

## Eugene Albert Fischer co-author

Fischer has a Bachelor's and a Master's degree in Economics. Upon graduating from college he spent one and a half years in a private Peace Corps organization, "Acción en Venezuela." Following this, Fischer and his Venezuelan wife spent four years in Honduras and Nicaragua with the U.S. State Department's Agency for International Development (AID). He then worked on Wall Street with F.I. DuPont as a security analyst. Subsequently, he developed and ran a series of small businesses beginning with Western

Union Computer Utilities followed by 17 years of successful maritime businesses in the Caribbean that included ship brokerage, ship ownership and operations, ocean salvage, and ship building and repair. He has been married to the former Imelda Sánchez Romero of Maracaibo, Venezuela for 47 years and they have four children and eight grandchildren. The Fischer household is multilingual speaking English, Spanish and some French.

Fischer has been incarcerated in federal prison since 1988, serving a life sentence on marijuana charges. His incarceration was based on a dry conspiracy with the testimony of cooperating witnesses. Fischer is a non-violent, first time offender. Since his incarceration, Fischer has earned his master's degree, become a Eucharistic Minister in the Catholic Church, become a lay member of the Discalced Secular Carmelites (a prayer order of the Catholic Church), has written two screenplays in addition to this book, and has served as an officer in the Jaycees, the NAACP, and Toastmasters. Fischer has taught educational courses for more than 20 years to thousands of inmates in GED and ACE (adult continuing education) courses, including Spanish, business principles, small business operations, business planning, personal finance, investments and various economics courses.

Fischer has no release date for his non-violent, first-time marijuana charge. He has continued to maintain his innocence of the charges but has been denied post-conviction, collateral relief even though his conviction was without a unanimous jury verdict and there were other serious irregularities in his trial.

This book is the result of the collaboration of Fischer and Parish and their teaching various economic courses together.

## Albert Eugene Parish co-author

Parish has a Bachelor of Science degree in both Mathematics and Economics and a Ph.D. in Mathematical Economics. While in graduate school, Parish taught undergraduate economics and mathematics students. Upon graduating, Parish became a college professor who taught in mathematics and economics departments at a state school. After 8 years, Parish moved to a private institution to help start an MBA program. He taught undergraduate and graduate students for 17 years. During this time, Parish became a well-known, highly regarded, regional economic forecaster, working with Chambers of Commerce and banks at the local, state and national levels. Parish has published numerous articles and had his own newspaper column.

Parish has a wife and four children who continue to provide support and love during his incarceration. Parish pled guilty to securities and internet fraud and is a first-time, non-violent offender. Despite these facts, Parish was sentenced to 292 months and will be eligible for release after serving 75 percent of his sentence. Parish's incarceration has harmed his family much more than himself.

While incarcerated, Parish has taught GED classes to Special Learning Needs students as well as Adult Continuing Education (ACE) and pre-release courses. Some of the courses he taught include Economics in the Media, Personal Finance, Employability, and Computer classes among many others.

Parish and Fischer met while teaching together and this book is a result of their friendship.

## Jesse Krimes Art Work

Krimes is an emerging artist from Lancaster, Pennsylvania known primarily for his contemporary sculptural work. He is a 2009 graduate from Millersville University with his Bachelor's Degree in Art. He was the sole proprietor and curator of Krimes against Metal Art Gallery, located on Gallery Row in Lancaster. Krimes' work has been featured in numerous exhibitions and publications as well as public works commissions. He is a non-violent offender currently serving a federal sentence of 70 months for drug distribution. He is projected to be released in March 2014 and will continue his artistic activities.

While incarcerated, Krimes has taught drawing and painting courses.

# Prologue

In a recent CNN broadcast of the television show GPS hosted by Fareed Zakaria, he made the comment that "the politicians didn't get it." On one hand, the Republicans were shouting that it was fiscal irresponsibility to spend a trillion dollars on a stimulus program as Barack Obama had done in 2008. Then, these same people were promoting renewing the Bush tax cuts at a cost of a trillion dollars. The argument was that Keynesian economic spending didn't work, that instead the Reagan approach of incentivizing the rich by tax breaks would stimulate economic growth and therefore bring in greater revenue to the federal government.

There is one thing wrong with this approach, as political analyst James Carville said, "The Bush tax cuts did nothing to stimulate the economy." Therefore, we are doubling up on a failed strategy." Ironically, Keynes, who is always quoted as promoting federal spending as the way out of recession, didn't advocate fiscal irresponsibility. He would have been the first to say there could be various and sundry ways out of a decline.

What he did advocate was for drastic measures in drastic situations, situations like the Great Depression of 1929-32 and like the Great Recession of 2007-10.

Most telling of all was the populist thinking in America at the end of 2010 that excessive taxation and the federal deficit were ruining America and, consequently, the federal budget had to be balanced at any cost. The mantra was that the profligacy of the federal government and America's thirty year deficit bankrupted the country and mortgaged the future of America's children and grandchildren.

On the GPS program, it was pointed out that China, as the largest foreign holder of U.S. federal debt and as a major partner for the production of consumer products for the U.S., was laughing all the way to the bank over the discussions the American public had concerning debt and taxes. Mr. Zakaria raised the matter increasingly asked by both friends and foes, "Just what are America's priorities? For it seems there are no long-term plans." How can the debate be fixed on fiscal austerity when the United States spent trillions of dollars on wars in Iraq and Afghanistan? How can the U.S. focus on the federal deficit as the cause rather than as one of the consequences of a thirty year binge?

While the U.S. is at a point of neurosis over the federal deficit and the ever-expanding federal debt, the Chinese are preparing to move to the next step of reinventing their manufacturing economy by spending one and a half trillion dollars in the next years on new green, environmentally friendly manufacturing.

The American economist Jeffrey Sachs stated, "The problem in the United States is that everything is short term, there is no long-term planning." It's an instant gratification society. The American public is conditioned as consumers to expect instant gratification and this carries out in its politics and in any attempt at national planning. While the Chinese look ahead for years and even decades, the United States is concerned with what's happening in the immediate future, this year or even this quarter or month.

After 30 years of a spending splurge not seen before in world history, the United States is facing some serious questions in the world community. It has depended on the rest of the world lending it money to cover a constant federal budgetary deficit. This has gone hand in hand with a trade deficit. So, those world economies with a trade surplus have lent the U.S. money to cover its continuous fiscal deficit. This has resulted in a massive federal debt which nearly exceeds its one year GDP (the total of all goods and services produced in the U.S.).

While this has occurred, the U.S. functioned in its role as the world's single superpower. This has entailed a cornucopia of wars to defend the U.S. and the rest of the world. The first and second World Wars placed the United States at the center of world power. They were devastatingly costly in men and funds. These were followed by wars against the communist threats and have morphed into a current situation of a war on terror manifested in military engagements in Iraq and Afghanistan which have now gone on for over ten years (in Afghanistan). Fighting wars have always been a costly affair but never as costly as modern warfare with its super weapons. It now costs a million dollars a year to keep a man fighting in the field.

The United States has approached its health care systems with a hodge-podge of programs from Medicare to Medicaid to prescription drugs for the elderly with no focus on a coordinated effort or total cost involved. If Social Security is added with current outlays projected as exceeding income, there just aren't enough monies coming in from tax receipts to fund everything. But then the public says we don't want to pay any more taxes. So where does the money come from. The U.S. says well we can borrow it. It is as if Americans believe it is their birthright to borrow and then borrow some more when they wish for something more. Any child psychologist would say that such behavior is immature and the child has to be told he can't just get whatever he wants, that priorities must be set, and that the child must live within limits.

The criminal justice system of the United States epitomizes this spend-thrift philosophy with its "lock-'em-up-and-throw-away-the-key" approach. While the federal government only bears a small part of the total, the states are burdened with huge expenditures to keep over two million men and women incarcerated, of which, the majority are non-violent and many are even first time offenders. And what are the benefits to the public? Does it really deter crime? Does it really make the average American safer? It seems to be the very example of a system in which costs far outweigh gains.

On the other side of the equation is the U.S.'s focus, or lack of focus, on education. While the Chinese and other countries are educating their young in mathematics and the sciences to the extent that they are head and shoulders above the same age group of young people in the U.S., there is no major U.S. national effort to improve public education. Presently, Asian American youths are ranked in the top 2 percent of developed nations with white youth ranked in the top 6 percent, black youth in the top 41 percent and Hispanic youth in the top 46 percent.

While students in China and India are spending more time in the class-room, American schools are looking for ways to reduce the class time of students to save money. With more than 50 percent of some high school students dropping out, there is a national emergency in American education.

If America spends $1,000,000 per soldier in Afghanistan and $50,000 per prison inmate per year, why can't America spend some of these resources on educating youth? America still has the best universities in the world but what will it matter if it doesn't have the primary and secondary schools to prepare its young to obtain college degrees?

There is much talk by American politicians of unfair labor policies and undervalued currencies giving other developing nations an unfair trade advantage. But what must be faced are two things: 1) that there will be currencies of trade and reserve other than U.S. dollar and 2) other countries will have rising labor forces which will earn considerably less than the average American laborer. But America can compete through innovation and productivity. While this increasing success on the part of the developing nations will displace some of America's industry and jobs, it does not have to signal an overall decline. Through its abilities to innovate, to create, to invent, and to bring new systems and products to market, America can continue to be a leading nation of the world. However, this will require new foci on national purpose, on education, and on research and development (R&D).

The United States and the U.S. dollar have had a major run in the 20th Century. The U.S. began the century as one of two superpowers and ended it as the only superpower. The U.S. dollar was the reserve currency of the world and all trade was figured in U.S. dollars. Globalization was promoted with the belief that more trade would always benefit the U.S. more than its trading partners. But it is natural that, as other countries prosper and their economies get increasingly strong, the U.S. will have to begin dealing with the nations of the world on a different basis - a basis of equals and partners, not subordinates.

The U.S. benefitted by the national pursuit of such things as space, the internet, micro circuitry, and personal computers. Without public investment, producers would not have become the leaders in world technology and the U.S. would not have been the 20th Century economic force that it was.

While it is true that private companies developed and expanded the products through private enterprise, without the government's initial investment, these products would not have come about. New efforts at R&D

must be developed by the U.S., first on a public basis then with the products turned over to private businesses that can bring them to market.

The United States must look at the world as a series of friends who are growing up and with whom the stage must be shared for the benefit of everyone. In other words, the world is a series of ships on the water and a rising tide will bring all the ships up - not just the big ones, nor the middle sized ones, nor the small ones by themselves but all the ships at the same time.

Other conventional areas open to rethinking and reconsideration in America in the new century are: (1) traditional housing in America (2) a multi-level labor force with a new policy toward low level immigrants and toward highly-trained, technically-oriented immigrants and (3) a new orientation as to saving, investment, and consumption. Questions of how the housing market should be restructured, with a change at least in part to rental from ownership to allow for the greater mobility needed in a job market in which Americans will be retrained and moved an average of about 7 times during their working careers, must be considered. Questions of how America focuses on its lower-end labor market, a market in which illegal immigrants now dominate in jobs few Americans will take at pay rates unacceptable to most Americans, must be considered. Such alternatives as worker permits, used in a country such as Germany, should be considered. A major new focus must be on how America lowers its consumption and increases its savings. It is improbable that the rest of the world will continue to willingly subsidize the American consumer with cheap money and a new economy will require the nation to reshape itself by saving to have the funds for investment.

Much is said about excess taxation in the United States but, as other countries demonstrate, it is not so much the tax rate as it is what the citizenry is getting for its taxes. The chant, "taxation without representation," spoke of another era and another set of circumstances. In colonial America, the problem was England taxed America and took the funds to England with little or no benefit to America. The United States taxation system has evolved into a convoluted and special interest system. It does not have the well-being of the nation at its center but too often seems to be geared to letting the wealthy keep their wealth. In December 2010, a group of the wealthiest Americans signed a petition declaring they would give back all their wealth for the public benefit. On the other hand, there is a powerful

American political movement to let the wealthiest pay lower or no taxes. By the end of 2010, the average tax rate to the middle class in America was the lowest in 20 years, taxes to the wealthiest one percent of Americans was exempted entirely in the case of estates, and income taxes for the top 10 percent was renewed at a 20 year low. The question must be asked, what does America want and what is it willing to pay for? Without some increases in taxation, much of current government must be curtailed. A cohesive, long-term policy must be pursued with taxation and realistic and affordable programs at its center. Without such mature policy planning, it is inevitable that the U.S. will have a major decline in the 21st Century. Only with a planned approach conditioned on what is feasible and what Americans are willing to pay for can U.S. national policy be successful.

The first decade of the 21st Century ended with America suffering from the worst recession in its history. The recession was brought on by two bubbles, "the housing bubble" and "the financial bubble." Both were products of unbridled greed and the lack of clear federal regulation. Self regulation was relied upon with the unrealistic belief that free market forces would control and rein in any excesses. Housing was expanded unrealistically with rampant speculation and largely un-policed and fabricated credit standards. Money was easy, flowing into the United States from all over the world. Coupled with this was a new Wall Street phenomenon called the credit derivative. Young whizzes came along and devised mathematical formulas showing derivatives could take the risk out of investing. An unholy alliance between credit rating agencies, Wall Street investment banks, and speculators reaped huge profits by promoting new investment units in which risk was traunched and slices of the new units were sold. But alas, the old fashioned statistical distribution of the bell curve prevailed and when one element started to unravel, the whole edifice collapsed. All of a sudden, banks and financial institutions were faced with catastrophic losses stemming from what were called sub-prime loans. Then America and the rest of the world found itself on the precipice of a very deep and dramatic financial collapse. The U.S. went into emergency mode, first with President Bush and then with President Obama and just barely managed to stem the hemorrhaging.

Then a surprising thing occurred in the new world order. China and the emerging nations pulled the world out of a global decline. The U.S. began to change structurally in both financial market regulations and the propping up of banks. But, it rapidly became evident that growth would be slow in resuming as the U.S. saw unemployment at 9.8 percent and GDP growth at anemic levels of 1.5 - 2 percent annually. A new order of things was apparent for the U.S. itself and in the communities of world countries. Europe experienced some real growth coming out of the recession then some of the peripheral countries in the Common Market had major sovereign debt problems and began to inaugurate a series of austerity programs by the end of 2010. This was mandated by the rules of the European Common Market. But who would mandate the U.S. to implement austerity measures?

In the U.S., neither political party is fully focused nor leading the American public along the road for real recovery. Unfortunately, short-term political goals seem to continue to dominate the American political scene. Those politicians who speak of fiscal responsibility and real growth oriented structural changes are either voted out of office or do not enjoy the support of their political parties. Even when a grass roots movement such as the Tea Party springs up, it tends to oversimplify and offer a negative program with little real growth restructuring. America must face the basic structural problems it has and devise a program with austerity measures but also prepare the country to compete in a new century.

We are not suggesting that big budget cuts or tax increases take place immediately. Sudden austerity would undoubtedly slow what has so far been a tepid recovery with high unemployment that is devastating families. We are suggesting changes necessary for the future and that the quicker a plan is made, the better off the nation will be.

This book explores facets of the American economy as it stands at the end of the second decade of the 21$^{st}$ century. Questions are raised as to the existing economic structure of the country and its federal government. It is indisputable that federal programs and a balanced federal budget must be rethought and changes must be implemented that will continue to place this country as a world leader. Either the U.S. makes the necessary changes on a voluntary basis or market forces will force the process. America must do what it has so often done in the past, restructure its economy and deal with other nations on an equal basis. Undisputedly, the next 100 years will be considerably different than the last one hundred. The 20th Century was an American century. The 21st Century will be a century in which the U.S. is an important and integral part of what is happening. It will probably not be the economic superpower it was. This does not necessarily mean America's standard of living will decrease. Rather, it means that the whole world will be improving with more nations entering the league of what is termed the developed nations.

# CHAPTER 1

# A REAL LOOK AT GDP

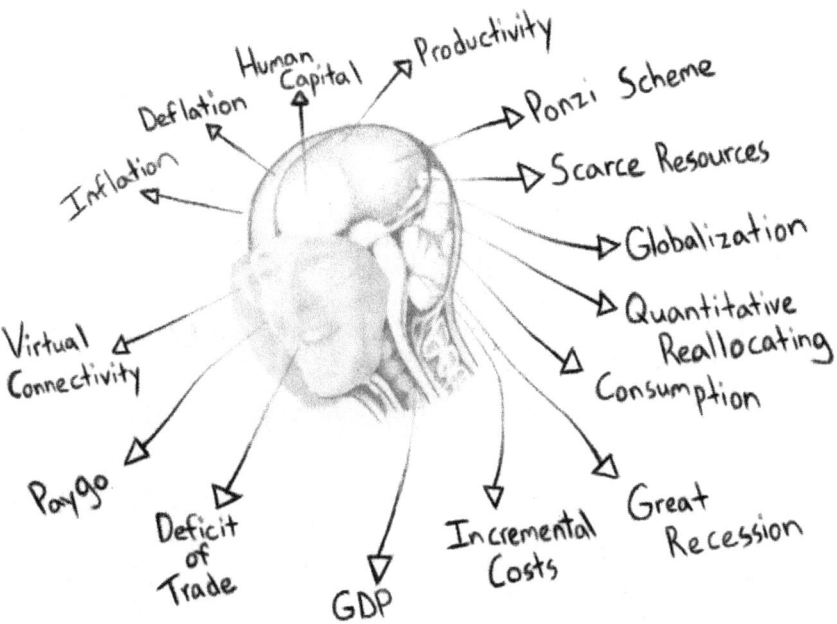

*"Thinking precisely and systematically about something as complex and irregular as a modern economy is very difficult, maybe impossible."*

ROBERT SOLOW

*"It takes a certain brashness to attack the accepted economic legends but none to perpetuate them."*

JOHN KENNETH GALBRAITH

*"Television has spread the habit of instant reaction and has stimulated the hope of instant result."*

ARTHUR SCHLESINGER

*"And we forget because we must, not because we will."*

MATTHEW ARNOLD

*"If you have to ask — shame on you"*

LOUIS ARMSTRONG

The U. S. economy is the largest in the world as measured by its gross domestic product (GDP). The standard definition of GDP is the total dollar value of all final goods and services produced within the nation's borders over one year. For 2010, the U.S. GDP was estimated at about $14.7 trillion, far more than that of any other nation and, in fact, about 25 percent of the total GDP of the world, in a nation with a population size of only about 5 percent of the world's population. Essentially, GDP measures the output of the nation over the course of a year, but it is worth taking a closer look at the definition and the components of GDP to gain a clearer understanding of what is - and what is not - being measured.

First, "total dollar value" indicates that U.S. GDP is measured in dollars, not euros, yen, yuan or pesos. Obviously, this is because the dollar is the currency of the United States. But other countries have measures of GDP as well, measured in their respective currencies. Britain's GDP is measured in pounds, Mexico's in pesos, Japan's in yen, China's in renmimbis, Brazil's in real's, and so on. When comparisons of GDP from one country to another are made, a conversion to a common currency is required.

Since the primary purpose of GDP is to measure output, a common measuring instrument is to use purchasing-power-parity to put the values of the outputs in comparable. In this manner, the ability of citizens to purchase goods and services are put in common terms and adjusted. For example, GDP is concerned with how many cars are produced in the U.S. versus China, and not the relative difficulty between an American and Chinese buyer in purchasing them. That is not to say this isn't important, just that it isn't what GDP measures.

Second, "final goods and services" refers to GDP's only counting goods and services used in their end purpose, not for the purpose of continuing intermediate production. For example, aluminum used to build a car is not counted in GDP but the car is. This avoids double counting.

Third, "within the nation's borders" implies that a good produced by a foreign company within the U.S. borders is counted in U.S. GDP while a good produced in a foreign country by a U.S. company is counted in the foreign country's GDP, not in the U.S.'s GDP. So a BMW car built in South Carolina by the German automaker counts in U.S. GDP. However, a Ford built in Canada counts in Canada's GDP.

Finally, "over one year" indicates that GDP is measured over a set period of time. In the U.S., it is reported quarterly but in annualized terms. It should be noted that such reporting of GDP is far from being a perfect measure of total output. For one thing, it totally ignores the "underground economy" which consists of both illegal activities such as drug trafficking and also legal but unreported activities such as restaurant tips or lawn mowing by a teenager. Furthermore, it doesn't count valuable but unpaid services like a housewife's keeping of a home and raising children. And, it does count some things that are paid for but have no real value. If Harry pays his neighbor Jim $100 to dig a hole in Harry's yard and then fill it in, and then Jim pays Harry $100 to do the same thing in Jim's yard, it would appear that GDP has grown by $200 but obviously economic growth has not occurred. Furthermore, GDP doesn't make any value judgments. Whether $1 billion is spent upgrading technology to make labor more productive in the work place or if it is spent making Disney World more enjoyable for vacationers, GDP rises by $1 billion in either case without regard to which choice makes society better off. In fact, economics usually avoids the difficult determination of what is truly productive and what is frivolous altogether until social welfare is considered.

In so much economics and finance, it is change in GDP that is the most useful measurement. The most common measure of economic growth is the real change in GDP, which is reported every quarter on an annualized basis. A report reading that real GDP grew by 2 percent in the third quarter of 2010 means that on an annualized basis, GDP rose by 2 percent after inflation. In essence, total output rose by 2 percent, discounting changes in prices. Of course, this doesn't mean that output of every good and service rose by 2 percent after inflation. There can be all kinds of variations in growth contained within the overall economy. For example, more apples could have been harvested than lettuce.

In a nation like the U.S. with the greatest GDP in excess of $14 trillion, a real growth rate of 4.5 percent implies dollar growth, after inflation, of $630 billion, a significant dollar sum to be sure. Because of the size of the U.S. economy, it is almost impossible to expect real growth rates at the 10 percent level of China, Singapore, or Brazil. However, most economists agree that rates of 3 percent to 5 percent are attainable and healthy in an economy of the size and maturity of the U.S. Unfortunately, the U.S. hasn't come close to these levels recently.

Another GDP measure often examined is GDP per capita, which is simply the total GDP divided by country's population size. It measures a society's output per person. While the U.S. by far has the largest GDP of all the nations, it is conspicuously behind in per capita GDP of other smaller nations such as Luxemburg, Norway, Iceland, Demark, Sweden, Switzerland, etc. But perspective shows that size controls. The size of the U.S. economy, based on total GDP and population size, is what controls the per capita GDP. Thus, nations such as China and India, with their huge populations will, with an expected doubling of their low per capita GDP in the next decade, become the largest economies in the world as they accomplish this per capita growth. However, they still have lower per capita GDPs than most other developed countries with smaller populations.

Per capita GDP is often used as a metric of standard of living and does allow a quick comparison of one country against another. With $14 trillion divided by 309 million, the per capita GDP of the U.S. is about $40,000, which places it 20th in the world. Luxembourg has per capita GDP of about $100,000, placing it first in the world. Obviously, this average doesn't show disparities and, in the U.S., we have a high percentage of the wealth in a small percentage of the population with 15 percent of the population earning below the poverty level. A country such as North Korea with the major part of its GDP in defense spending will show a real distortion when per capita GDP is considered. While its per capita GDP will rank it within parameters of favorable showing of many other nations, because of its distortion of spending, its people are close to starvation.

In 1990, the United National Development Program published another measure called the Human Development Index. It combined two other indicators, adult literacy and life expectancy with income levels to give a better overall index. In 1991, years of education was added to this calculation. It showed the United States as ranking 13th worldwide. In one part of this human development factor, in that of gender differences, the United States only ranked 19th. With the present crisis in education, as described more fully later in this book, all indications are that the U.S. will slip even further in this overall human development test. Even the Heritage Foundation's Economic Freedom Index rates the U.S. as only 8th in the world.

## GDP Components

GDP is also broken down into its components that provide a useful profile of how output is spread among those with an economic claim to it. There are four broad components to GDP. The first is consumption, which includes all goods and services bought by citizens with the exception of housing. Consumption includes items like groceries, gasoline, clothing and haircuts - that is, items which are typically thought of as being consumed. Also, items like tuition, appliances, and medical care are considered consumption items. Consumption is further broken down into services and goods, and goods are further broken down into durable and non-durable goods. Durable goods like appliances last more than more than one year while non-durable like spring flowers for the patio last less than a year. In the U.S., consumption accounts for about 70 percent of GDP, around $10 trillion. This ratio rose over time and economists refer to the consumer spending as the backbone of the economy. This level of consumption is higher than that of most other developed countries. High consumption leads to a buffering of the effects of recessions, which decrease growth but only rarely result in outright declines in consumption. The Great Recession of 2007-2010 is an exception.

The second component of GDP is government spending, including federal, state, and local levels. Government spending includes all operational spending such as salaries and wages for police, teachers, and public employees. Capital spending such as for new schools, highways, and firehouses is also included.

The third component of GDP is gross private domestic investment that includes spending on plant, capital equipment and technology by businesses, and on housing by households. This category does not include spending on capital equipment, plant, or technology by government. This component of GDP accounts for 18 percent of the total, or about $2.5 trillion. It is this component where long run economic productivity first begins.

Labor becomes more productive over time with technological progress and with more modern capital equipment. As an example, the computer/internet age has been the major stimulus for the surge of economic growth in the last two decades. Businesses invest in research and development (R&D), capital equipment, and plant expansion when aggregate demand for products and services is rising. Such investment leads to expansion of productive capacity. If demand is slack, existing capacity will be sufficient and investment spending will decline. Such decreases postpone economic growth in the long run.

The fourth component is net exports, which is the difference between exports by the U.S. to its trading partners and imports into the U.S. from its trading partners. The U.S. was a net exporter until about 30 years ago and now consistently runs a deficit of trade, in excess of $700 billion per year. U.S. exports of goods, services, and income account for about 12 percent of GDP, while U.S. imports are about 17 percent of GDP. So, U.S. net exports are negative 5 percent of GDP. With this long term deficit, the U.S. has actually had its GDP reduced. This phenomenon is a natural result of globalization, i.e. cheaper goods come in from low wage countries while high wage countries must specialize in more technological and capital intensive goods production. However, because of this globalization, this categorization is more difficult to measure. A Honda Accord built in Ohio and sold in Kansas is not an import even though profit goes to a Japanese company. In all these transactions, buyers purchase imports because they want to for a combination of price and/or quality.

## GDP Inputs

The flow of output just described in GDP calculations is matched by a flow of money to the inputs of production that produce the output. The largest of these is labor which receives wages and salaries. Owners of land and natural resources receive what economists call rent. Owners of capital receive interest and business owners receive profits. Government collects taxes and our trading partners receive currency. The banking system coordinates these flows of output and money by providing credit to "grease the economic engine." During the Great Recession, the near collapse of the banking system was the equivalent of dumping sand in the engine, which would have wrecked the economy and precipitated an outright depression. In the Great Recession of 2007-09, it was stated, as it was during the Great Depression of 1929-32, "that things could have been worse." While this doesn't provide any comfort to workers, businesses, or retirees who were severely impacted economically by these two events, it nevertheless is probably true.

## Three Economic Questions

The three economic questions that the U.S. faces at this moment are the same ones it has always faced, but they have special significance at this juncture in the economic history of the U.S. They are: 1) How much and what types of output can we (and do we want) to produce? 2) How do we produce them? and 3) For whom do we produce them? The world, and especially the U.S., is swept up in a revolution of technological progress. This revolution has brought many other nations along in a very rapid pace of development. In turn, this very development has placed tremendous strains on the world's resources. There is ever more competition for scarce natural and other resources. It is critical that the U.S. understand the dynamics of this new world and its own place, both its limitations and its advantages, in this world. Rather than a philosophy of Helter Skelter planning, the country must make intelligent and well thought out decisions to adjust and to progress in this new world. This will mean choosing between alternatives and utilizing with efficiency the "in-some-ways-abundant-but-in-other-ways-limited" resources of the U.S. and interacting in a world of increasingly equal partners.

# CHAPTER II

# Debt In America

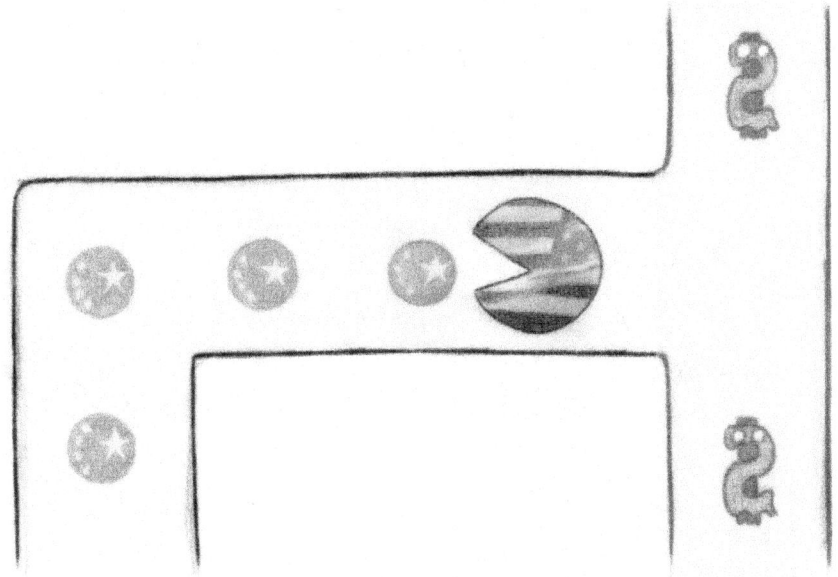

Debt In America
(Pacman Phenomenon)

*"The USA is the only country ever to go the poorhouse in an automobile."*
WILL ROGERS

*"I shall be telling with a sigh somewhere ages and ages hence, two roads diverged in a wood, and I, I took the one less traveled by, and that has made all the difference."*
ROBERT FROST

*"Every civilization that has ever existed has ultimately collapsed."*
HENRY KISSINGER

J ust when the politicians tell the people it is alright, that we just had a cyclical glitch, it then becomes worse. America has been living beyond its means for 30 years now and has swept the rest of world along in its wake. It is like a Pac-man game where you keep gobbling up dots to win and, in the end there is no more, the dots are all gone. So America's deficits are being gobbled up in purchases of debt and in the end there will be nothing.

By the end of 2011, the twin deficits of the federal budget and the trade deficit were at an all-time high of $2 trillion. We speak of them together for the budget deficit is covered by the dollars the U.S. exports to import foreign goods, which in turn are lent to cover the federal budget deficit. This has placed China, which has become the United States of America's factory, in the position of being the biggest holder of American Treasury bonds. China now has foreign exchange reserves of more than $1.5 trillion and is a partner with the United States in wanting to maintain the dollar's strength.

## America's Debt

The United States has gone through at least three "binges" in the past three decades: the internet bubble, the housing bubble, and the financial instruments bubble. And underlying all of them has been the explosion of debt. As of the end of 2009, the U.S. owed over $35.5 trillion in debt broken down as shown in Figure 1.

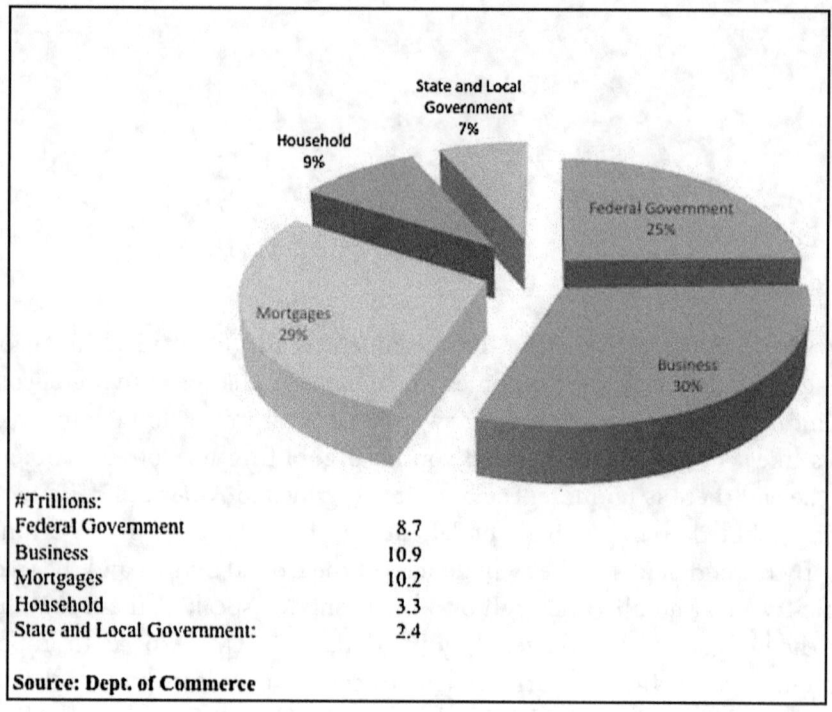

Fig 1 Total US Non-Financial debt outstanding

In order to try and limit federal debt, the U.S. Congress has imposed a debt ceiling that the government cannot exceed without permission from Congress. Presently, that ceiling is at $14.294 trillion. As can be seen from Figure 2, this ceiling has been continuously raised in the last 30 years, even during the Clinton presidency when there was a surplus in the federal budget.

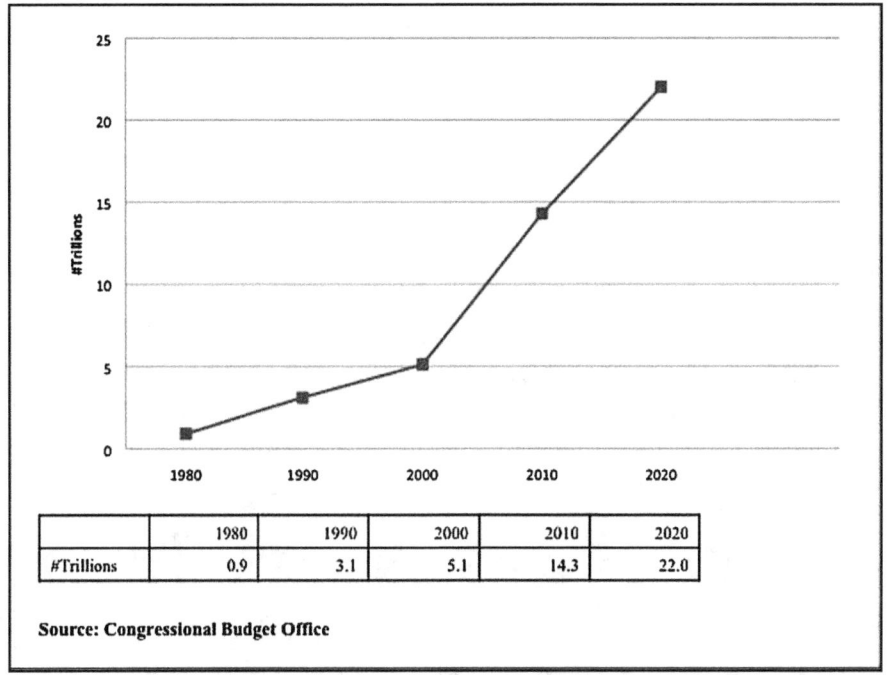

| | 1980 | 1990 | 2000 | 2010 | 2020 |
|---|---|---|---|---|---|
| #Trillions | 0.9 | 3.1 | 5.1 | 14.3 | 22.0 |

Source: Congressional Budget Office

Fig 2. Growth in the Federal Debt Ceiling, # Trillions

Figure 3 illustrates when the federal debt of $14.3 as of mid 2011. Two points are clear, both worrisome. First, at $6.1 Trillion added to the debt over his 8 years, President George W. Bush's total exceeded the total of all prior administrations in the nation's history by about $200 billion! At current rates of increase, President Obama is on track to beat President Bush's dubious record by adding at least $10 trillion to the debt if he should serve two terms.

Second, the amount of US debt held by foreigners is rising, especially now that Social Security about 'breaks even' annually. Foreigners hold $4.5 trillion currently, just under a third of the total. US government entities hold a total of $6.2 trillion, leaving $8.1 trillion in so called 'public debt'. Foreigners own over half the public debt. The debt held by US government entities will have to be repaid from general revenues when needed. And at a low 2% average interest rate on foreign debt, a full $90 billion is paid to foreign debt holders each year. When interest rates eventually rise, so will this figure. That's $90 billion per year, roughly the annual cuts in the recent debt ceiling deal, sent out of the country. Of course these interest payments do come back to the US – as further debt purchases requiring our nation to pay interest on the interest we just paid! Of our foreign debt holders, China, Japan, and Great Britain are the top three.

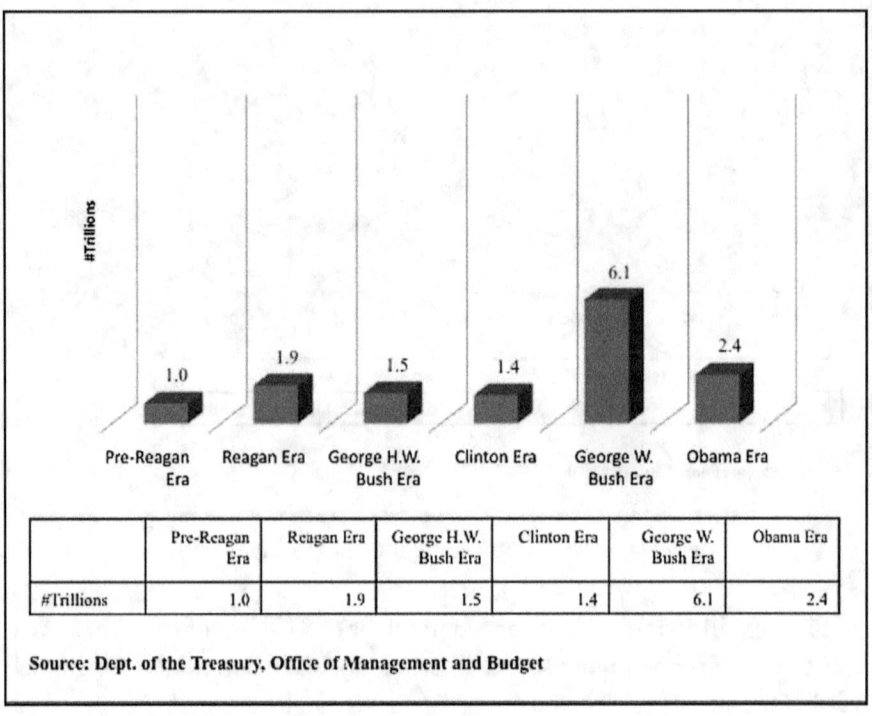

| | Pre-Reagan Era | Reagan Era | George H.W. Bush Era | Clinton Era | George W. Bush Era | Obama Era |
|---|---|---|---|---|---|---|
| #Trillions | 1.0 | 1.9 | 1.5 | 1.4 | 6.1 | 2.4 |

Source: Dept. of the Treasury, Office of Management and Budget

Fig 3a Contributions to the federal debt, trillions mid 2011

# Federal Deficit

The federal budget deficit is the difference between what the government gets in revenue and what it spends on federal programs. When the federal fiscal year ended on September 30, 2010, the federal deficit stood at $1.3 trillion, or 9 percent of GDP, the second largest since World War II (the largest was in the prior fiscal year). While this figure reflects the effects of the recession and the temporary stimulus program, both of which are fading, it does suggest a bleak near-term future. Based on current policies, the Congressional Budget Office (CBO) has estimated the federal debt, which is now 62 percent of GDP, will rise to 87 percent by 2020. If state and local government borrowing is added in, the total will be about 110 percent of GDP. This debt increases because of federal budget deficits. The federal debt is just the accumulated federal deficits of the past.

In the European Common Market, the United States could not meet the criteria for remaining in the union because its deficit exceeds the maximum allowed 3 percent of GDP. Of course, some European Common Market countries like Portugal, Ireland, Greece, and Spain don't currently meet this requirement either. For the past three decades, the United States had a federal budgetary deficit in all ten year spans except three of the Clinton presidency years. Projections are dismal with the CBO projecting an annual deficit up through the year 2035. Although, no one should believe a 25-year economic forecast!

The International Monetary Fund (IMF) has stated that America's structural deficit and its uncontrolled debt over the medium term are among the worst in the developed world. And unfortunately, the IMF states that the U.S. doesn't appear to have any plan to change this scenario. Of the rich nations, Germany recently passed a balanced budget constitutional amendment and Britain's coalition government started an ambitious four year austerity program in attempt to slash its massive deficit. Even France has raised its retirement age, trying to rein in social overhead spending. Greece is still a mess despite its austerity programs.

In the present environment, America has the excuse that the economic recovery is still too nascent. Economic growth in the second half of 2010 was a dismal 2 percent annual rate and unemployment has been over 8 percent with little near-term prospects of change. Some are predicting that if taxes rise significantly or spending falls, the economy could slide back into recession as happened to Japan in 1977.

On the other hand, there are political reasons why America is not reacting. Principally is the fact America has never been an austerity oriented country. As Gene Steuerle, a scholar at the Urban Institute, said, America's fiscal policy has alternated between "giveaways" and "takeaways." The post World War II period, from 1946 through 1981, was an era of giveaways in the U.S. This was exemplified by the expansion of entitlements (programs that have to be continuously maintained once established) in such areas as Medicare and Medicaid in 1965. Then in 1982, President Ronald Reagan flipped to takeaways by cutting taxes. However, along with the tax reduction, Reagan also began the massive defense buildup that characterized his political philosophy. These policies produced a massive structural budget deficit with the 1981-1982 recession as a result.

## Federal Budget

In federal budgeting, there are two conflicting sides: entitlement spending and discretionary spending. Entitlement areas are required spending by law. The biggest items are Social Security, Medicare, and Medicaid. Unless Congress changes the law, these programs must be funded because the American people have been led to believe they are entitled to the involved benefits. The other programs, which are the great majority in number of federal programs, are not required programs but are discretionary programs that depend on Congress each year. These include almost everything else in federal spending such as defense, education, justice, infrastructure, and the sundry other federal programs.

### In the 2010 U.S. federal budget expenditures were:

Social Security ............................................ 20 percent
Medicare/Medicaid .................................... 22 percent
Defense.................................................... 19 percent
Interest on Debt ........................................ 7 percent
Discretionary ............................................ 33 percent
(nondefense)

The federal budget in fiscal year (FY) 2010 amounted to $3.7 trillion but revenues coming in were $2.4 trillion, thus producing a deficit of $1.3 trillion. A glimpse of the budget breakdown as summarized in Figure 4 shows that any attempt to solve the imbalance completely from the spending side requires some very difficult choices. Since discretionary spending is only 33 percent of the total, it is almost certain that major reductions will also have to be made to the entitlement side of the budget in order to get it in balance.

The entitlement budgetary items have a long political history in the United States, starting with the Social Security Act of 1935 and running through the 1944 G.I. Bill of Rights, the 1956 Social Security Disability Benefits Act, the 1962 Child Welfare Program, the 1965 passage of Medicare and Medicaid, the 1974 Food Stamps Program and the Supplemental Security Program for the aged, the 1974 Special Supplemental Program for women, children and infants, the 1997 State Children's Health Insurance Program, and most recently the Obama health care overhaul and the Pell Grant expansion.

Since 1983, when 29.6 percent of Americans received some form of government benefits, this number grew to over 44.4 percent by 2008. Even with this increase, the U.S. population, on average, lived on a lower amount of government benefits than citizens of other developed countries.

## The Big Entitlements

While Social Security is presently functioning (barely) in the black and the government is actually using the Social Security monies for other budgetary purposes, it will not be long before it also will be functioning at an annual deficit. For FY 2011 and FY 2012, the payroll tax reduction passed to stimulate the economy further exacerbated Social Security's fiscal situation. As outlined in the chapter on Social Security, the long term viability of the program requires that structural changes be made.

With the other big three budget items of Medicare, Medicaid, and defense, some cuts must be made in any attempt to balance the federal budget. The following figures show how the national outlays for defense and for Medicare have soared. See Figures 5 and 6.

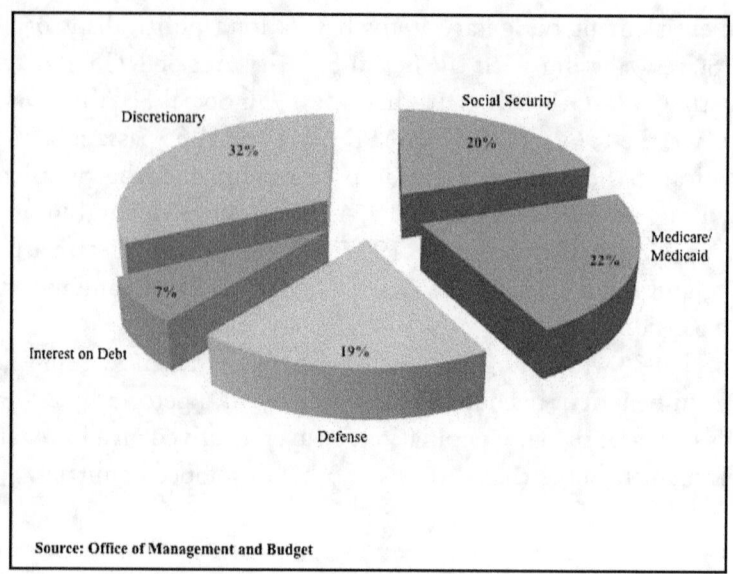

Fig 4. Fy 2010 budget expenditures, % of total

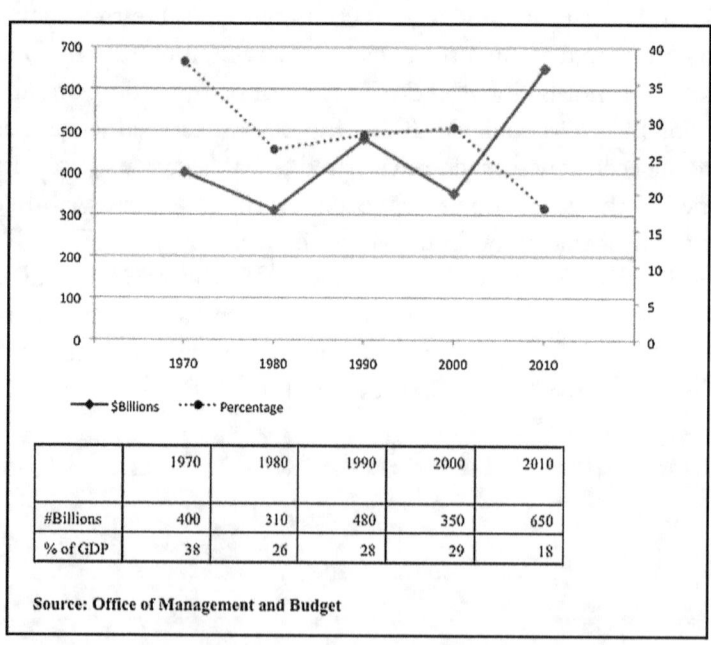

|  | 1970 | 1980 | 1990 | 2000 | 2010 |
|---|---|---|---|---|---|
| #Billions | 400 | 310 | 480 | 350 | 650 |
| % of GDP | 38 | 26 | 28 | 29 | 18 |

Source: Office of Management and Budget

Fig 5. Defense expenditures growth

In addition to the outlay of some $700 billion annually for defense, there are war allocations which Congress makes off-budget to continue wars in Iraq and Afghanistan. These bring the totals for the defense closer to the trillion dollar mark.

Former Defense Secretary Robert Gates suggested that changes in contract methodology and bidding be made to eliminate some of the fat in the defense budget. Also, some long-term programs such as the very expensive Stealth fighters and bombers must be closely analyzed with the view of limiting them, if budget balance is to be achieved. While defense is not entitlement per se, it is treated as such in political reality. Serious study must be done on a non-political basis to determine just what is really needed to keep America safe. This will undoubtedly lead to the closing of many overseas bases and U.S. commitments that should be handled by allies.

Health care, both the existing Medicare and Medicaid and the newly passed Obama health insurance changes, will have to be examined to see where reductions can be made by such methods as co-pays, larger deductibles, etc. The new "Obamacare" was passed as budget neutral, not increasing federal spending in its implementation. Medicare and Medicaid each exceeded $600 billion in the FY 2010 budget. With present trends of health care inflation of almost 9 percent annually, these programs will grow at about 3 times the projected GDP growth. Improved administration and cost savings can slow down some of this growth and will be necessary to reduce overall budgetary deficit numbers. But more will be required.

## Taxes and the Federal Budget

There are three ways to balance the federal budget: 1) decrease spending, 2) increase revenues, and 3) increase the size of the U.S. economy thereby increasing the tax base.

Notwithstanding political rhetoric, tax rates have increased in America under both major parties in the years 1982, 1983, 1984, 1987, 1990 and 1993. While there was an attempt to eliminate many exemptions in 1986, America's tax code is still very cumbersome and is riddled with loopholes. If tax loopholes were eliminated, there could be about $1 trillion added to revenues annually.

Some attempts have been made to rein in excesses. In 1983, a bipartisan effort was made to cut Social Security benefits, to gradually increase the retirement age, and to implement a higher payroll tax on Social Security. Then in 1996, President Clinton and a Republican Congress reworked welfare to limit long time recipients and put more responsibility on state governments.

Congress passed the Budget Enforcement Act of 1990 which placed limits on discretionary spending. The "Paygo" rule required any tax cut to be offset by a spending cut. Dovetailing this, any increase in entitlements had to be offset by a corresponding tax increase. These measures resulted in a slowing of the rate of deficit increases.

Unfortunately, American politicians have a short memory and uncontrolled fiscal policy began again. For this reason, the Balanced Budget Act was passed with the goal of balancing the budget by 2002. However, a surge of revenue occurred that brought the budget in balance for fiscal years 1998, 1999, and 2000 under President Clinton. Under President Bush, taxes were cut on income in 2001 as well as on capital gains and dividends in 2003. The first big entitlement in years was signed in 2003 for Medicare prescription drug benefits and in 2002 Paygo lapsed. This all resulted in the budget once again returning to a deficit. The amazing thing is that, through all of these deficit years, the international bond market didn't seem to care about what appeared to be America's propensity to spend beyond its means as the U.S. continued to borrow at low rates.

# Global Savings and America's Deficit

Throughout the past 30 years, the world has used the U.S. dollar as the currency of reserve. After the World Wars, with the disappearance of the gold standard, the dollar was used by a country to maintain its monetary reserves and was the backbone of the international currency system.

Even with, or possibly because of, the continuous U.S. federal deficits, there was no end to people's and nation's willingness to lend the U.S. money by purchasing its Treasury bonds. The glut of global savings in the 1990's went, in part, into the U.S. Treasury bond market. This and the desirability of the dollar kept interest rates low. The United States has a record of never defaulting on any of its federal debt but that could change.

In the 21st Century, with other economic power blocks developing such as China, India, Brazil, and the European Common Market, this situation is evolving into something different. The recent crisis in the European countries of Portugal, Ireland, Greece, and Spain (euphemistically called PIGS) shows that fiscal control is being increasingly required and rewarded. The banking crisis of 2008-09 shows on a worldwide basis, including the United States, that even the most revered and apparently stable private companies and financial institutions can be mismanaged and brought to collapse. It is not beyond reason to believe that unless the U.S. gets its fiscal house in order, borrowing rates will increase dramatically to compensate for what the market will qualify as a higher risk. The once sacrosanct dollar lost its triple AAA rating in the third quarter of 2010.

At present unsustainable levels of deficits, the U.S. will be spending from 25 percent to 50 percent of its federal budget on the servicing of its debt within the next 20 years. This is fiscal insanity and will in itself signal the collapse of the dollar as the international currency of choice.

## Where We Stand Today?

As this book is written, a major nightmare is unfolding in Washington corridors. The federal government is approaching its debt ceiling. By law, this is the maximum the government can borrow to run itself. This ceiling is approached every year because the continuing deficit produces the need to continue to borrow. The challenge is coming from a new political force called the Tea Party. They helped to elect a number of new Congressional representatives who are demanding serious cuts in the federal budget before any increase be made to the federal debt ceiling. What could the consequences of any delay in raising the ceiling be? The reason the United States can refinance its federal debt instruments is that they are sought after. There never has been a default in paying such instruments. World markets believe that there is absolute security in such instruments and therefore world markets purchase everything the U.S. issues and interest rates remain extremely favorable.

If there is any threat to such repayment of debt, the credit worthiness of U.S. federal debt instruments could be downgraded. Such a downgrading recently occurred in Europe. Its effects would be twofold, one in liquidity, i.e. in issuing and redeeming such instruments and, second, in interest rates charged. If any of the major credit grading agencies downgrade America's AAA status, debt service cost would increase from 6 to 7 percent of the federal budget to higher numbers. It is conceivable that, with the present trend in financing, an ever-increasing federal deficit, and the possibility of higher interest rates needed to float this credit, the percentage of the federal budget to pay interest could double to 12 to 14 percent. This would exacerbate the problem by forcing further cutbacks in other government programs in order to meet past debt obligations.

Countries such as Argentina and Russia have had similar problems and it wrecked havoc on their ability to draw international capital. In today's liquid world, the free movement of capital is necessary. Any change to the credit worthiness of the U.S. and its currency would have devastating effects on the world economy as well as the U.S. economy.

# CHAPTER III

# THE FEDERAL DEFICIT

*"The cure for this ill is not to sit still or browse with a book by the fire, but to take a large hoe and a shovel also and to dig till you perspire."*

RUDYARD KIPLING

*"The end may justify the means, as long as there is something which justifies the end."*

LEON TROTSKY

*"Great God! This is an awful place and terrible enough for us to have labored to it without the reward of priority."*

ROBERT FALCON SCOTT

The United States is drowning in red ink. Our federal deficit and debt are so out of control that the public and most economists are frightened to death. Right now, the deficit exceeds $1 trillion, a figure that many economists are projecting will continue for the foreseeable future. When we speak of the federal deficit, we simply mean that the total money taken in from taxes is less than the total we are spending on all federal programs. Common sense will tell you that you can't spend more than you take in, at least not for a continued period of time. If an individual person, household, or company does it, they end up bankrupt. Just recently, Greece got so bad in the European Common Market that people were forecasting it was heading for disaster and would probably bring down the rest of the European Common Market with it. Greece's federal deficit had reached the level of almost 11 percent of its GDP. To maintain Common Market status, the maximum allowed is 3 percent. For fiscal year 2010, the United States reached almost 10 percent. In other words, the United States was at a level of ailing Greece and, if it had been part of the European Common Market, might even have been expelled from that illustrious group.

The politicians are telling the American public that some level of federal deficit is permissible and even desirous. To determine the truth, one only has to do some analysis of the economic history of the United States. Traditionally, the United States functioned on a pay-as-you-go basis. Up to the last 30 years, except in times of war such as World War II, the United States had a federal budget which was near balance with receipts. This was considered good fiscal management. Even when the necessities of extraordinary wartime spending such as WW II ballooned the federal budget to almost 20 percent of GDP, the country was rapid in correcting this situation once the war ended and it was in balance within several years. In the last decades of the 20th Century, fiscal control jettisoned and the United States began to function at a deficit, or in other words, politicians began spending more money in programs than was entering the coffers of the

Treasury. People such as Ross Perot began to speak up and tell the country that this was total insanity and irresponsibility. But, in the end, there was no will to cut programs. It was as if people were saying, "Well, yeah it is wrong, but don't cut funding of this road project, or this system of federal medical insurance, or these unemployment benefits." The words were spoken but the political will was not there to make the necessary changes, the required austerity measures. And to make matters worse, there was no one to criticize or force the United States into line, such as the case of Greece and less powerful countries. Who would dare challenge the United States and, even if another organization or country were to do so, the United States would pay them no attention or even seek redress from the party daring to do so.

The consequences of these deficits, of this fiscal profligacy, can either be significantly increased inflation with currency devaluation or a dramatic increase in public debt. The United States had a brief period of high inflation but, in general, has faced its deficit problem by issuing Treasury debt - largely because the dollar has been considered the safest currency in the world. It has been relatively easy to get both United States and foreign investors to buy the debt instruments issued to cover these deficits. However, as is always the case, anything which covers the problem but doesn't resolve or cure it will eventually have negative consequences. Presently, due to the last 30 years of deficits, with the rare surplus situation of the Clinton years, the accumulated public debt has reached $8.5 trillion in 2010 and swells to over $15 trillion when debt the government owes itself, such as to the Social Security trust fund, is factored. This is where this dramatic increase in public debt begins to really kick in. Projections are now that federal spending will be about 25 percent of GDP while federal revenues are projected at about 19 percent, a deficit of 5 percent. Using Office of Management and Budget figures, this deficit level, if unresolved, will result in unsustainable interest levels with some pessimistic projections that they may become as much as 25 percent of the federal budget within 10 years. It can see such a level will become impossible to sustain with consequences of lowering of the United States' credit rating or even the eventual lowering of the standard of living of the average American.

There are two broad ways of reducing or eliminating this budget deficit and to begin to pay down the accumulated debt such as individual households are in fact doing with the unsustainable debt levels they had coming out of the Great Recession contraction of 2007-10. The first way is to reduce spending. The second is to increase revenues. Either way requires making hard choices, some of which will have immediate, short-term, negative economic and social consequences before the long-term, positive consequences are realized.

In analyzing the problem, we must start with one fact that is unusual about federal accounting terminology. If we suppose that last year's budget for a specific program was $1 billion and this year's budget is projected at $1.25 billion, but that the actual figure for this year came in at $1.1 billion, then politicians claim a cut of $150 million, a decrease of 12 percent, instead of what is really an increase of $100 million or 10 percent. By this use of terminology, the politicians hide the truth. They claim decreases to budgets when in fact they are only decreases to projected increases. To begin to resolve the problem requires real reductions, not just political-speak. The simple truth of the matter is that any intelligent person could eliminate the deficit with one hour of work. Of course, this would require a non-political environment and non-politicians and that is why Congress doesn't seem to be able to fix the problem of what programs to cut and what revenue to raise.

From the spending side, Social Security, Medicare and Medicaid, defense and interest on the national debt are the big items, totaling 68 percent of the budget, and projected to be over 100 percent within 10 years unless changes are made. Interest on the national debt is largely out of the government's control. It can only be reduced by reducing the level of debt and that requires completely eliminating the deficit or reducing the interest rate paid, which is largely controlled by global markets. As of 2010, the average rate was a low 1.2 percent. With an estimated 60 percent of federal debt coming up for refinancing within three years, these favorable rates will probably continue. However, such low rates are just temporary and will only increase in future years. Furthermore, the very high level of U.S. debt will probably in itself lead to significant increases in the rates the markets will require to finance what is considered reckless deficit spending.

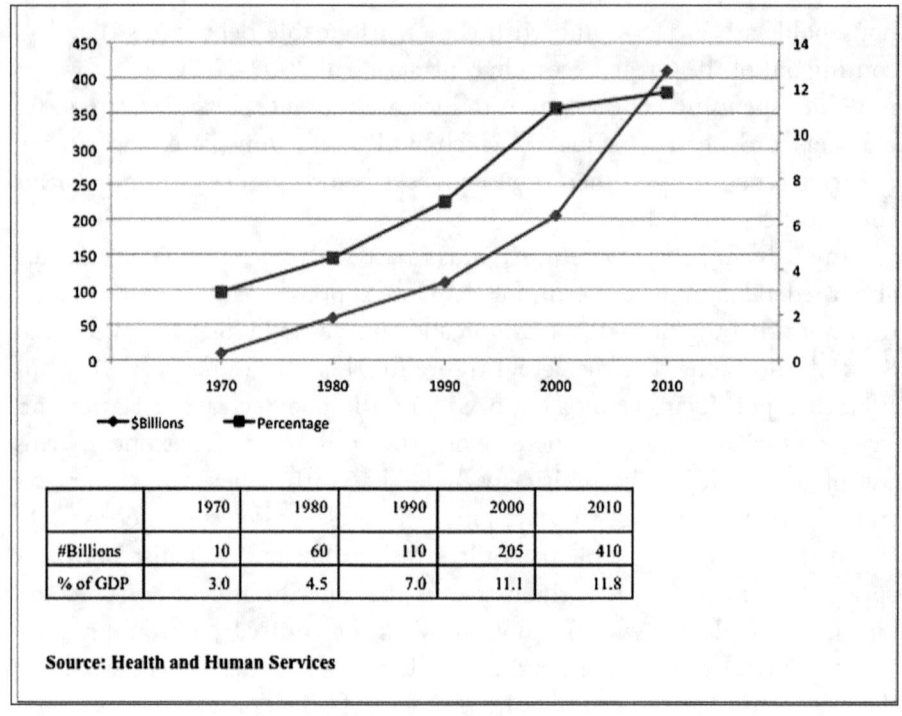

| | 1970 | 1980 | 1990 | 2000 | 2010 |
|---|---|---|---|---|---|
| #Billions | 10 | 60 | 110 | 205 | 410 |
| % of GDP | 3.0 | 4.5 | 7.0 | 11.1 | 11.8 |

**Source: Health and Human Services**

Fig 6. Medicare expenditures growth

So what's to be cut? Social Security and Medicare-Medicaid are covered more fully in other chapters that go into depth concerning the long-term prospects of these programs and their inherent instability. Defense is the other major item and also will be discussed in depth in a later chapter, but it exemplifies the need for the United States to make some hard choices and the willingness of the American public to pay for what the program is offering. The U.S. spends in excess of $700 billion per year on defense, representing almost 20 percent of the budget and 5 percent or greater of GDP. This is without including special off-line expenses for financing wars, such as Iraq and Afghanistan. What makes this number really significant is that it's greater than the combined spending of the rest of the world. As can be expected, when a budget gets so big, there are major inefficiencies and redundancies. U.S. defense spending is so big that in itself, it surpasses many countries' GDPs. Defense expenditures can be cut or reduced to save billions of dollars, but it will necessitate some hard choices. Bases across the United States will have to be closed, contracts with defense contractors cancelled, foreign bases closed, and troops brought back home. In making these decisions, there are hard questions to be asked of the necessary defense level of the country and what can and should the American public pay for maintaining it. If the past is any indication, defense cuts will be met with strong opposition. However, never has the United States been in the financial straits as it is now.

The United States spends about $1.2 trillion on other programs such as education, housing, welfare, energy, transportation, foreign aid, its judicial system, and now what has been initiated in a very expensive homeland security program. The total spent in these programs is only 33 percent of the federal budget and even if they all were eliminated, the budget would still be in deficit. Nevertheless, certain parts of these programs should be modified to reduce inefficiencies and waste. When attempting to do this, past experience indicates there will be political resistance since every line item will have a constituency.

One reform that should be made, and for which there should be no disagreement, is to split the federal budget into capital and operating components. Presently, there generally is no distinction and thus capital investments are expensed out as regular expenditures. This would never be done in the business world where expenses are current while capital investments are expensed out by depreciation and amortization over their longer term useful life. Simply put, bridges and highways have a longer life than office supplies and should be treated quite differently in financial terms. The authors of this book believe that a more realistic approach would be to use a net present value approach when making capital expenditures. Then the hard quantitative test would be whether a project's NPV is negative or positive. Only projects with positive NPVs would be approved for funding. This is management on a cost-benefit basis, something which government rarely does now. In using such approaches, the United States would begin to run itself on a professional basis and only undertake projects which could be shown to offer positive results. The United States would return to being a country run on a pay-as-you-go basis.

As to operational spending, some reductions will occur automatically with economic growth. For example, unemployment compensation falls with sufficient employment growth. However, with estimates of near-term growth of the economy pessimistically compared to previous growth, it is unlikely that the economic push given by such growth in the past will reoccur in the foreseeable future. Other savings will be possible with more professional management, such as comparison shopping and competitive bidding with few or no exemptions but will not be the sea change needed to get us out of the deficit position. This was exemplified by President Obama's call to make significant efficiency changes in the 2011 federal budget but only resulted in the savings of a few $100 million, less than .5 of 1 percent of the federal budget.

On the revenue side, increasing revenue can occur through economic growth, unit tax rate and fee increases, or through new kinds of taxes or fees. Of these, economic growth is the most economically, socially, and politically easy to accept.

Higher economic growth, especially if it comes with increases in employment, will automatically increase some tax revenues such as personal and corporate income taxes. Higher growth will reduce some federal spending and thus also reduce the deficit. The problem is that it appears the economic growth of the U.S. economy will be more restricted than in past recoveries. Most economists believe there is no realistic scenario under which output and employment will rise by a sufficient percentage for the nation to grow its way out of the deficit. Thus, GDP growth can only be part of the revenue side of reducing the deficit - not the total solution, no matter how appealing it is for politicians to say this is the solution to the U.S. predicament.

The revenue decisions will amount to raising tax rates or imposing new taxes. These decisions can be presented in the guise of "tax reform." But, in order to get past the emotional reaction of terminology with political connotations, it would be beneficial if the nation asked and answered the very basic question of what is the purpose of the tax system. The answer should be the primary purpose of taxation is to raise revenue to fund government spending. However, in the American system another purpose is to enact social policy, by reallocating scarce resources. For example, the deductibility of mortgage interest results in more capital and labor going into construction than would otherwise be the case if market forces were the only ones involved. Another example is the deductibility of charitable donations. These increase such giving, which is considered a desirable social function. Deductions as the oil depletion allowance have stimulated investment in oil exploration which might not otherwise have occurred with the aim of diminishing dependence on other nations for our oil energy needs. So the question becomes whether the U.S. tax system should be used to encourage or discourage economic and social decisions or should it be exclusively used to raise revenues? Tax reform and the balancing of the federal budget are much simpler if only the revenue raising function is the focus.

In the present U.S. tax system, unit tax rates can be raised on income, including wages, capital gains, dividends, interest, etc. Higher rates will have consequences in that the action of taxpayers affected will lead to actions to mitigate such increases. Amounts and persons affected will vary depending upon the amount of rate increase and to what it applies. Rolle's Theorem from calculus can give us a basis for calculating possible consequences. Applying the theorem to tax policy, we see that if the tax rate is 0 percent, no tax revenues are collected. If, on the other hand, the rate is 100 percent, there will also be no tax revenues, except in the short-term because there will be no reason to continue the activity being taxed. Figure 7 shows Rolle's Theorem applied to tax rates versus tax revenues:

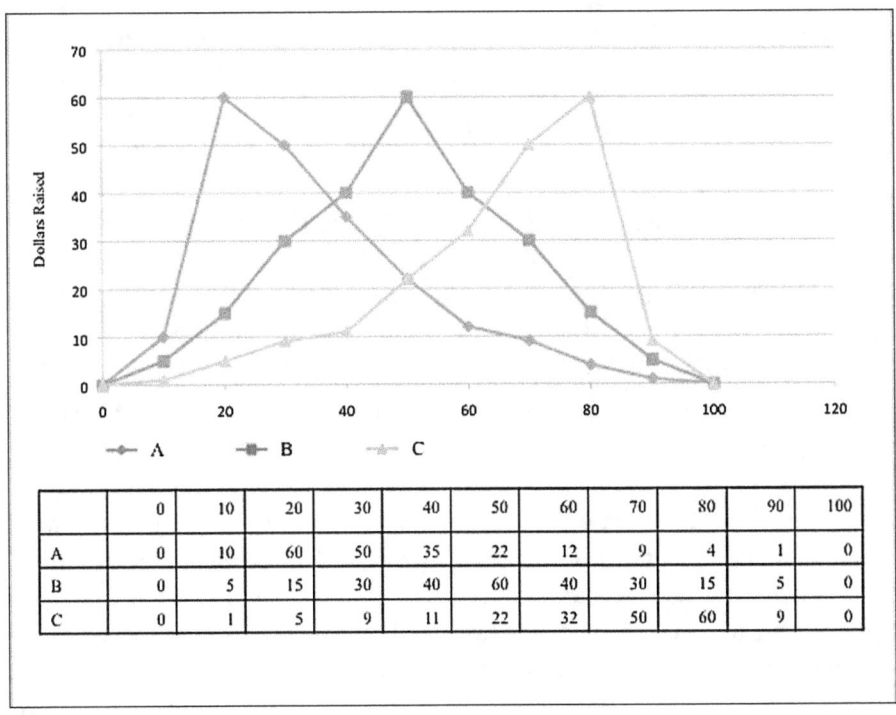

| | 0 | 10 | 20 | 30 | 40 | 50 | 60 | 70 | 80 | 90 | 100 |
|---|---|---|---|---|---|---|---|---|---|---|---|
| A | 0 | 10 | 60 | 50 | 35 | 22 | 12 | 9 | 4 | 1 | 0 |
| B | 0 | 5 | 15 | 30 | 40 | 60 | 40 | 30 | 15 | 5 | 0 |
| C | 0 | 1 | 5 | 9 | 11 | 22 | 32 | 50 | 60 | 9 | 0 |

Fig 7. Rolle Theorem

In each curve, points 1) and 2) illustrate the 0 percent and 100 percent rates. The issue then is what tax rate is revenue maximized for a given economic activity? For curve A, it is about 20 percent as higher rates reduce revenues quickly. Capital gains are a probable example of this alternative. For curve B, the rate is about 50 percent and for curve C, it is 80 percent. In the best management sense, research would be undertaken to determine the optimal tax rates for each activity. In actuality, the U.S. tax code applies different rates to different activities but not optimally, and certainly not with a rational analysis of cost/benefit and budget management.

New taxes are also an alternative, although one that the U.S. public has not seemed to want to consider. A commonly mentioned one is the value added tax (VAT), which is used extensively in Europe. VAT operates as a stealth national sales tax as it is hidden within the price of a good. Suppose the value added in the production of a loaf of bread is $2. A 10 percent VAT would mean the bread would sell for $2.20, the sales price of the bread. In other words, the VAT is not added at the cash register as with an ordinary sales tax. VAT can raise billions of dollars in revenue but it would be costly to implement since it is collected at every stage of production. It must also be noted that each dollar of VAT reduces the income available for consumption by one dollar. VAT can also be raised at any time without the consumer directly knowing it is being charged due to its stealth nature. In other words, the consumer doesn't know whether the price of the bread rose from a VAT increase or from the price of wheat going up.

A national sales tax is another possible consumption tax that would be an alternative to a VAT tax. It operates the same way in raising prices but is collected at checkout, making it more transparent to the consumer. The "fair tax" was an example proposed that contained a national sales tax but was proposed as an alternative to, as opposed to an addition to, both income and FICA taxes.

In either of these tax options, the new tax targets consumption, which represents 70 percent of GDP. These taxes would discourage consumption. It would be necessary to replace any lost economic activity with government spending, export increases, and additional investment to offset the economic slowdown that might be produced. Too often, government fails to consider that any increase in taxes represents a transfer of money from those who pay taxes to the government. The real question then becomes who does the money belong to anyway? In our democratic society, it is assumed that it belongs to the people in the final analysis.

So the focus must become on what services do the people of the United States want government to provide and how will these services be paid for. These really are questions of allocating our scarce resources in the most intelligent and well thought out way possible. But the American public has been led to believe, or maybe the politicians really believe, that there are no limits and the U.S. can have ever-increasing services without paying ever-greater taxes. The present situation is unsustainable and the taxpayer is beginning to perceive this.

# CHAPTER IV

# TAXATION

*"The income tax return has made more liars out of the American people than golf has."*

WILL ROGERS

*"The best politics is good government."*

ADLAI STEVENSON

*"Doublethink means the power to hold two contradictory beliefs in one mind simultaneously and accept both of them.'*

GEORGE ORWELL

L ocal, state, and federal governments receive funding from taxes and fees paid to them. Tax policy can be based on either the ability-to-pay or benefits-received systems. Under an ability-to-pay system, those subject to the tax - who are more able to afford it - pay more without regard to how much benefit is derived from the services funded by the revenue. For example, a homeowner pays property taxes on his home to fund public schools whether or not he has children in public schools and the higher-valued the home, the greater the dollar amount of tax depending upon the particular area. The implied assumption is that the owner of a more highly-valued home can afford higher property taxes – an assumption that is not always valid.

Under a benefits-received system, the person using the service funded by the tax revenue pays for it. For example, a bridge toll is paid by the drivers who cross the bridge. Those drivers who do not use the bridge do not pay the toll. Similarly, licensing is based on the benefit-received principle. A driver's license, hunting or fishing license, or business license is paid for by drivers, hunters or fishermen, or business owners, respectively. The question then becomes which system should be used and why?

Broadly categorized, taxes fall into three classes: property, sales, and income taxes. The federal government receives income taxes from both individuals and from corporations. It also collects sales taxes in the form of excise taxes, from purchasers of particular products like alcoholic beverages, gasoline, or tobacco. The federal government does not collect property taxes.

Most states and some localities collect sales and income taxes. All collect property taxes. Generally, property taxes are the most stable source of revenue. As the housing bubble has shown, property values can and do fluctuate. However, historically they have not fluctuated as much as income tax revenue has, which is more sensitive to economic growth and job creation. During the Great Recession, households reduced purchases of goods and services, especially durable goods and vacations, in favor of debt reduction. Consequently, sales tax revenues declined across the country and plunged in most tourism-dependent areas, so sales tax revenues fell even more than those from income taxes.

The problem for governments across the nation is that the Great Recession was precipitated by a housing bubble that reduced property tax revenues. With the ensuing debt crisis and cutback in spending, sales tax revenues also dropped precipitously. Then with rapidly rising unemployment, income tax revenues fell with the consequent problem of an increase in job insecurity and consumer sales fell again producing a further fall in sales tax revenues. Collaterally, with consumer spending down, savings began to rise. This pushed many governments - federal, state and local - to deficit levels. In order to reduce these deficits – a necessity with the state and local governments and something which the federal government should do – tax revenues must be increased. There is a school of thought that increasing taxes in a recession has negative effects. The thinking is that natural GDP growth will bring tax revenues up again. The problem is, since GDP growth is down and tax revenues are down, there will be an increased deficit because government spending does not decrease parallel to the decrease in GDP.

Increasing tax or fee revenue is referred to as "revenue enhancement" by politicians since it sounds more politically appealing than "tax increases." And there is a difference between raising tax rates and raising tax revenues – a difference often deliberately missed by politicians. Consider a county that imposes a property tax averaging 1 percent of assessed value on all property. Suppose that in 2007 the assessed value was $250 million but that the bursting of the housing bubble caused the assessed value to drop to $200 million, unfortunately a realistic 20 percent decrease. Property tax revenues would then have fallen from $2.5 million to $2 million, also down 20 percent. There would be three possibilities to raise tax revenues. One would be to wait for economic growth to push assessed values back to $250 million, a turnaround which would probably take years. The second is for construction to rise so that the number of properties increases and thus the total assessment value of properties increases. The theory is that once

$50 million of new construction occurs, property tax revenues will recover the $2.5 million shortfall. The problem with this is that, in most parts of the United States, there is an excess supply of homes and a recovery in construction will take years to develop. Either of these alternatives would increase tax revenues without raising the tax rates. The third alternative is to actually raise the tax rate. By increasing the property tax rate from 1 percent to 1.25 percent of assessed value, the revenue raised on the lower assessed value of $200 million will rise back to the $2.5 million level. The problem with this approach is that it has the politically disastrous result of a tax increase of 25 percent.

The problem with property tax increases during an economic downturn is that a homeowner with a $150,000 home used to pay $1,500 in property taxes. If that homeowner knows his home's value has dropped by 20 percent to $120,000, he is expecting a property tax bill of $1,200 as oppose to $1,500. Even worse, if this homeowner's home value has not fallen at all – and not every home will fall in the same amount or percentage even in the same block – his new tax bill could rise to $1,875. The problem is that the homeowner's income probably has not risen by 25 percent, or even worse, he may have lost his job. He will not be a very happy voter, especially if he feels the country is wasting money or spending it unwisely.

When politicians claim they won't vote to raise taxes, they are really talking about tax rates. If such a policy is pursued, the only way for revenues to rise is through economic growth in general which raises the tax base in particular. In the realm of income taxes, this requires higher taxable income or an increase in number of income earners.

One way to obtain higher taxable income is to eliminate deductions from gross income. The wage earner does not have any more income but the amount of that income is subject to income tax increases. Make no mistakes, while this is not a tax rate increase (since no change in rates occurs), it is a tax increase (since tax revenue paid by a household rises). Here are some deductions that could be eliminated with an estimate of the amount of additional tax revenue raised per year:

| | |
|---|---|
| Eliminate mortgage interest deduction | $ 88 billion |
| Eliminate charitable donations deduction | 47 |
| Eliminate state and local tax deduction | 78 |
| Tax investment income (dividends, capital gains, interest) at ordinary income rate | 24 |
| Tax value of retirement account (401K and IRA) contributions | 118 |
| Tax value of employer-paid health insurance premiums and health care | <u>131</u> |
| | $486 billion |

These changes raise almost one-half trillion dollars a year, cutting the deficit by about one-third. Each one has a strong constituency that would not want it changed. Some politicians want to make such changes in the name of "simplifying the tax code" but would reduce rates simultaneously so no additional revenue is raised. This wouldn't help the deficit but would reduce the misallocation.

Another possible means of changing the revenue generated from taxation would be to raise the wages subject to Social Security withholding taxes from the current $106,800 to a higher figure such as $190,000. If such an increase were enacted along with the lowering of the benefits for higher income people and increasing the age to qualify for full benefits, there could be a saving of as much as $238 billion annually and a prolonging of the solvency of the Social Security system.

Sales tax revenues can be raised by increasing rates as many states and localities have done or by expanding the goods and services to which sales taxes apply, which also has been done by many states and localities to help balance budgets. It must be remembered that the state and local governments must balance their budgets in that they can't simply print money as the federal government can to cover a budgetary deficit. The broadening of the sales-taxable base to include goods, such as newspapers, and services such, as doctor office visits, is being considered in many regions around the country with some controversy due to the regressive nature of sales taxes.

Any tax can be measured against income as progressive, proportional, or regressive. A progressive tax is one in which the percentage of income paid toward the tax rises with income. A household with taxable income of $50,000 might pay $10,000 in income taxes, 20 percent of income while a household with $100,000 of income might pay $30,000, 30 percent of income. In a progressive tax, the percentage of income rises with income, not just the dollar amount of the tax.

With a proportional tax, the percentage of income paid toward the tax stays the same with the income. A flat income tax would be proportional. Thus, with a 20 percent flat tax, a family with a $50,000 taxable income would pay $10,000 while a family with a $100,000 income would pay $20,000, the same 20 percent in both cases. Note that, while the percentage is the same, the family with the higher income pays double the amount of taxes because its income is double the lower earning household's. In a progressive system, the amount a higher earning family would pay is more than the percentage difference in earnings.

Under the unlikely assumption that incomes and house values rise together, property taxes would also increase if incomes rose. Thus, if a homeowner pays 1 percent of the value of a $150,000 home in property taxes, the tax would be $1,500. If the homeowner's income is $50,000, the tax of $1,500 would be 3 percent of income. With the $100,000 income household, the property tax on the same home would be proportional only if the home value was $300,000. Since home values and income aren't directly proportional, this is highly unlikely and the percentage of property tax would be higher on the lower income family. This would be a regressive tax.

Sales taxes are regressive even though the sales tax rate applied to the dollar purchase stays the same. Suppose, for example, that a county has a 5 percent sales tax and the $50,000 income family spends $30,000 on taxable purchases. It would pay $1,500 in sales taxes, which is 5 percent of the amount spent but only 3 percent of income. If the 100,000 income household spends $40,000 in taxable purchases, it pays $2,000 in sales taxes. But, this is only 2 percent of its income rather than 3 percent as for the lower income family. Thus an interesting phenomenon occurs: as the household's income rises in dollar terms, the dollars spent on goods and services rises also but falls as a percentage of income. A low-income household may spend all of its income on necessities, making 100 percent of its income subject to sales taxes. But the higher-income family will not pay as big a percentage of income in tax because it will spend less than its entire income on such goods and services.

Most politicians and economists, though certainly not all, favor a progressive tax system while polls show that the public believes a proportional system is the fairest. Current political discussion centers around making the income tax system "flatter." "Flattening" the income tax reduces the marginal tax rates across all income levels by reducing or eliminating deductions. But remember that each set of deductions has its own supporters (lobbyists). Such a system would have the result of being a less progressive income tax system. On the other hand, a value-added system would be regressive for the same reason a regular sales tax is, i.e. lower income households spend a greater percentage of income than higher income ones.

While corporate and individual income taxes comprise the greatest share, it should be noted that the present situation has favored the corporations over the past ten years. Between 1996 and 2000, more than 60 percent of corporations paid no federal taxes whatsoever. Even with the soaring profits of the last 15 years, corporate tax receipts fell to just 7.4 percent of overall federal tax receipts in 2003, the lowest level since 1983 and the second lowest since 1934. It should also be noted that the General Accounting Office (GAO) found 94 percent of corporations reported less than 5 percent of their total income subject to taxes during this 1996-2000 period. What then are the corporations actually paying in federal taxes? Corporate tax receipts dropped from an average of 4.8 percent of GDP in the 1950s to 1.3 percent of GDP in FY 2003. Thus, while the top statutory corporate tax rate was 35 percent, the actual share of corporate profits paid in taxes since 1993 has been just 25 percent. Furthermore, tax loopholes to corporations reduced revenues by $177 billion for FY2002 through FY2006 - $44 billion in 2002, $53 billion in 2003, $64 billion in 2004 and $16 billion in 2005. As corporate tax receipts decreased, payroll taxes increased dramatically. From 1.6 percent of GDP in FY 1950, they increased to 6.8 percent of GDP in FY 2002 and actually surpassed both corporate income taxes and excise taxes by FY 2002, an increase which brought their contribution to federal revenues up 30 percent. As of FY 2009, there was an estimate that corporate tax loopholes were "costing the American public" over $50 billion annually (Citizens for Tax Justice).

While corporate income taxes were falling as a percentage of GDP over the past half century, individual income taxes rose from 5.8 percent of GDP in FY 1950 to 8.3 percent of GDP by FY 2002.

The following changes could raise nearly $100 billion annually from corporations. The real issue is whether we want to use the tax code to encourage research and development or investment in plant and equipment, even if it reallocated resources.

| | |
|---|---:|
| Eliminate accelerated depreciation deduction | $56 billion |
| Eliminate research and development credit | 6 |
| Tax deferred income on foreign operations | <u>32</u> |
| | $94 billion |

There is a move in Congress to look at changes like these but only in return for a lower tax rate on U.S. corporations to make the rate closer to those of our global competitors. Economically, it is true that corporate profits are doubly-taxed, once from the corporations and once from the shareholder when profits are paid out as dividends. A strong argument can be made that either profits are taxed at the corporate level or dividends be taxed at the shareholder level, but not both.

Reform will be needed to change the size of taxes collected. While higher tax receipts can come from a higher effective tax rate and the percentage of the pie contributed by the different entities described, it will take some type of tax increases in rates to begin to close the federal fiscal deficit. There is validity to the premise that increasing the total economy through overall growth will also help to close the fiscal deficit but it is highly improbable that such increased growth alone will be enough and will come fast enough to make a serious dent in the deficit.

One of the issues of taxation has been that 'the rich pay more." But frequent polls have shown that a question like "if a taxpayer earning $50,000 per year pay $5000 in taxes, how much should a taxpayer earning $500,000 per year pay?" is usually answered by "$50,000." Of course, the taxpayer earning $50,000 would pay closer to $150,000 with our progressive system. "Fairness" to the average citizen means "equal share" and that translates to proportional, not progressive. Figures 8 and 9 illustrate the distribution of income and income taxes 20 years ago and now.

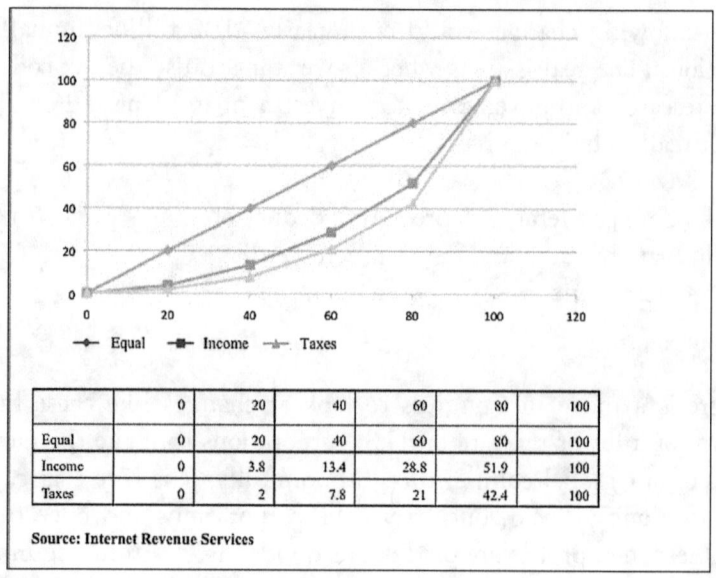

| | 0 | 20 | 40 | 60 | 80 | 100 |
|---|---|---|---|---|---|---|
| Equal | 0 | 20 | 40 | 60 | 80 | 100 |
| Income | 0 | 3.8 | 13.4 | 28.8 | 51.9 | 100 |
| Taxes | 0 | 2 | 7.8 | 21 | 42.4 | 100 |

Source: Internet Revenue Services

Fig 8 Income and tax distribution 1990

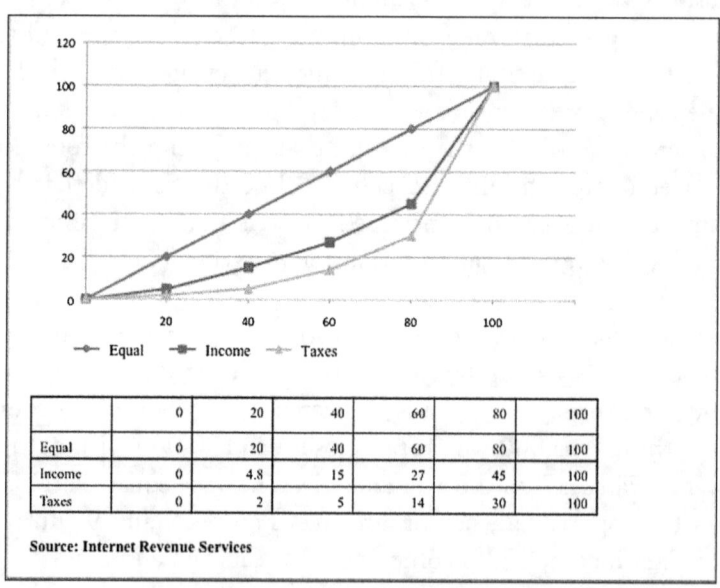

| | 0 | 20 | 40 | 60 | 80 | 100 |
|---|---|---|---|---|---|---|
| Equal | 0 | 20 | 40 | 60 | 80 | 100 |
| Income | 0 | 4.8 | 15 | 27 | 45 | 100 |
| Taxes | 0 | 2 | 5 | 14 | 30 | 100 |

Source: Internet Revenue Services

Fig 9 Current income and tax distribution

In both figures, the straight lines represent equal distributions of income and taxes. In these distributions, each quintile (20 percent) of households pays 20 percent of taxes and receives 20 percent of income. Twenty years ago, as shown in Figure 8, the distributions of income and taxes were equal. In particular, the top 20 percent earned about 50 percent of income and paid 60 percent of income taxes. Today, the top 20 percent earns about 55 percent of income and pays 70 percent of taxes. The distribution of income is more unequal than it was 20 years ago – the rich got richer. But the rich also pay even more in taxes than they did 20 years ago. A "soak the rich" mentality simply will not raise enough money to solve our deficit problems. New tax rules to encourage the rich to invest more in businesses will increase employment and that will generate more income tax from everybody, helping to solve two problems simultaneously.

Twenty years ago, the bottom 50 percent paid 18 percent in taxes and earned 20 percent of the income. Today, the bottom earns 20 percent of income and pays 10 percent of taxes – no income gains but less in taxes.

## Present Situation as to Taxation

Debate on taxation has been suspended because of the Great Recession. Traditional wisdom is to not raise taxes in an economic downswing. However, it is more than probable that there will have to be some tax increase to bring down the federal deficit. In December 2010, the Obama administration proposed a compromise to Congress with an extension of the tax decreases that the Bush administration implemented. Such a rescinding of these tax decreases would have, in essence, been an increase in taxes. Central to the discussion was the extension of the lowered taxation rare of the very rich. The Republicans presented the view that, during a recession, any tax increase would be wrong. The alternative to a general rescinding of tax decreases of the Bush administration was just to bring the tax rate of the very rich back to pre-Bush rates. The compromise was to extend the Bush tax decreases to all people for another two years. The additional revenue to be received by return to the pre-Bush tax rate for the wealthy would have been in excess of one trillion dollars over a ten year period, a significant number for a nation attempting to balance the federal budget. Again, this assumes the wealthy would not change their behavior, probably incorrect.

That such tax increases would dissuade capital from being invested in the U.S. is the principle argument against any such change. One school of thought is the wealthy and most entrepreneurs are not dissuaded from investing at tax rates such as those presently used or even by what appears to be the rates that would go into effect if pre-Bush rates were re-imposed. In fact, an argument could be made that the lower Bush-imposed tax rates did little to stimulate the U.S. economy and, in fact, the economy was more dynamic under the Clinton presidency with higher tax rates of the era.

As suggested in this chapter - loophole elimination, adjustments to Social Security withholding taxes (especially as it pertains to the very wealthy), adjustments such as changing the capital gains taxes, disallowing the deduction of mortgage interest charges from income for tax purposes - would significantly increase taxes collected. Such changes would be borne by almost all strata of the economy and would probably be the least painful politically.

In summary, the authors of this book would suggest that increased tax revenues from a recovering American economy in the next several years will be well short of sufficient to meet budgetary needs. While expense cuts will have to be made, it is inevitable that some form of tax increases will also have to be implemented.

# CHAPTER V

# DEFENSE

*"War is the continuation of policy, with the admixture of other means."*
                    KARL PHILLIPPE CLAUSWITZ


*"All warfare is based on deception."*
                                        SUN TZU


*"It is well that war is so terrible: we should grow too fond of it."*
                                        ROBERT LEE


*"There is no instance of country having benefitted from prolonged warfare."*
                                        SUN TZU


*"The most persistent sound that reverberates through man's history is the beating of war drums."*
                                        ARTHUR KOESTLER


*"Mankind must put an end to war, or war will put an end to mankind."*
                                        JOHN F. KENNEDY

The United States is the world's only remaining superpower and, as such, it is also the world's policeman. During the time of the British Empire in the 19th Century, it was said that the sun never set on the Commonwealth. Today, it can be said that the sun never sets on American troops. The U.S. has troops and bases all over the world. Since the end of World War II, America has maintained bases in Germany and Japan, the losers of the war. Since Korea, the United States has maintained a presence there, some 35 years. Of course, there was pride in the United States saying this presence prevented the resurrection of the military forces of both Japan and Germany. These nations were regarded as naturally belligerent. The estimated 4 to 5 percent of GDP these two countries would be spending on a defense went toward economic recuperation, and there is a valid case to be made that such spending was a major impetus in their recoveries. In Korea, the war was fought over the fear of Communist intrusion from China. And once won, in part, the U.S. had to continue with an occupational force. In Vietnam, the war was fought, after the French lost its Indochina conflict, to prevent the domino effect of another country falling to the Communists. Unfortunately, the war was a disaster for the U.S. and the Vietcong took over the country with Communism being the economic-political system.

The United States of America was born in violence. The first war was the Revolutionary War against the British, where the colonists fought a guerrilla war and won. It was difficult and costly but the British, with their traditional formations, were soundly beaten. It was in the best sense a war for a good cause, for liberty to self-rule. Following this victory, the United States went about the job of nation building. The historians, the Beards, put it succinctly: democracy flourished because the country had the immense job of colonizing the vast frontier. But, during the next 100 years, after such events as the Louisiana Purchase from France, the country came to a halt in its westward expansion, stopped by the Pacific. All the energies of the infant nation went into this great expansion, so began the outside wars. When settlers in what became Texas, Arizona, New Mexico, and even Southern California pushed for annexation to the United States, the United States engaged in a war with Mexico. While this fighting was spoken of in idealistic terms, it was really about new possessions for the United States. The aforementioned states were annexed from Mexico as a result of the fighting. In 1861, a bloody civil war, in which over 500,000 men were killed, was fought between the North and South. The United States engaged the British again in the War of 1812 because Britain was shanghaiing American sailors. Next was the Spanish-American-Cuban War, fought with Spain. The outcome was the annexation of Puerto Rico from Spain and the temporary management of the Philippines by the United States. In the 20th century, a series of new conflicts with the United States squarely in the middle developed: World War I and II, Korea, Vietnam, Panama, Nicaragua, Iraq, and Afghanistan as well as a series of lesser skirmishes such as Bosnia and Sudan. Some were clearly fought under the mantle of stopping Communism while others were simply to safeguard the world from further violence. But the latest conflicts were under a new banner, "a war on terrorism." For the first time, it could not be stated that there was a clearly foreseeable end strategy in sight as this war on terrorism had no clear enemy.

So what is the effective and necessary level of military spending for a nation? This answer depends on a series of factors:

1) the status of the nation in the power structure of the world's nations,
2) the perceived and actual dangers to the nation from other nations or forces,
3) the economic condition of the country,
4) the fiscal condition of the country, and
5) the international treaties and commitments of the county.

Concerning these factors, the United States has an enviable position but also a heavy burden, being the world's only superpower. As pointed out by Paul Kennedy in his book "The Rise and Fall of the Great Powers," while a country's military power flows from its economic strength, its decline is also directly related to its expenditures. The great empires going back to the Greeks under Alexander, to the Roman Empire, to the Ottoman empire, to the British empire, to Germany under Hitler, to Communism and the U.S.S.R., all had their day of military superiority but all also had their declines. While it may be debated which came first, the overall economic decline of the nation or its military decline, one thing is certain: world empires have required immense spending to maintain their military superiority. As Kennedy pointed out, military spending to maintain a world superpower position cannot be sustained perpetually. There always comes a moment when it is simply too onerous for the superpower. Thus, we saw the decline of the U.S.S.R. coming when an America, under the presidency of Ronald Reagan, pushed the U.S.S. R. to the brink in an arms race. The U.S.S.R., to maintain its military power on a par with the U.S., had to spend an estimated 20 percent of its GDP - an amount that devastated that country. But the United States, in order to keep the pressure on the U.S.S.R., also increased its defense spending significantly to levels not seen since World War II. While this put serious strains on the U.S.S.R., resulting in its collapse under Communism, it also put the U.S. in a serious deficit position in its federal budget. The presidency of Bill Clinton worked to balance its budget and seriously cut military expenditures. This threatened vested interests such as armament companies with their lobbyists. So, with the ensuing presidency of George W. Bush, the U.S. began to increase military spending again. Then after the attack on the Twin Towers in New York on 9/11/01, there was a new reason to upgrade military spending. The wars with Iraq and Afghanistan followed. Although the alleged charge of "weapons of mass destruction" being stockpiled by Saddam Hussein was later disproved, it nevertheless was adequate provocation to go to war. This stimulated the second war with Iraq, the first being Desert Storm fought over Kuwait during the presidency of George H.W. Bush. Then the U.S. invaded Afghanistan over the provocation that Bin Laden, the ringleader of Al Qaeda, was hiding in its mountains. While victory in Iraq seemed so easy with the military force of the U.S. overriding that country in days, final victory has been elusive for an insurgency developed which fought a guerrilla-tactics conflict. American hawks have given the new battle cry of fighting terrorism to this new conflict, a substitute for the theme of the many years of the Cold War of fighting Communism.

So what is the outcome of all this fighting? There have been positive factors that came from the bloodshed by America in its many conflicts.

Freedom from England, the elimination of slavery, and the stopping of several tyrants including Hitler, Hussein, and Bin Laden - who were on a course for world destruction - have all resulted from America's military exploits. On the other hand, the costs in lives and the effects on the federal budget have been great. With a defense budget of over $700 billion, America spends more militarily than the aggregate spending on defense of the allied countries. This figure does not include special off-line appropriations made to support a war as it is being fought. With these expenditures in recent years, the real figure is in excess of $1 trillion annually. Another factor, rarely understood by the American public, is the costs of individual fighting men to the U.S. Supplemental spending in both Iraq and Afghanistan have reached $1 million annually to put each American soldier in the field. The continued monetary expenditures caused by fighting wars, which was only realized 50 years after World War II, will probably be another $1 trillion for the medical costs of returning solders over their remaining life times, a cost the nation must morally assume. Through 2011, the U.S. cycled more than 2,000,000 fighting men and women through the wars in Iraq and Afghanistan.

## World Comparison of Defense Spending

Although the U.S. spends considerably more than any other country on its defense, the number of troops of some of the leading countries are shown in Figure 10.

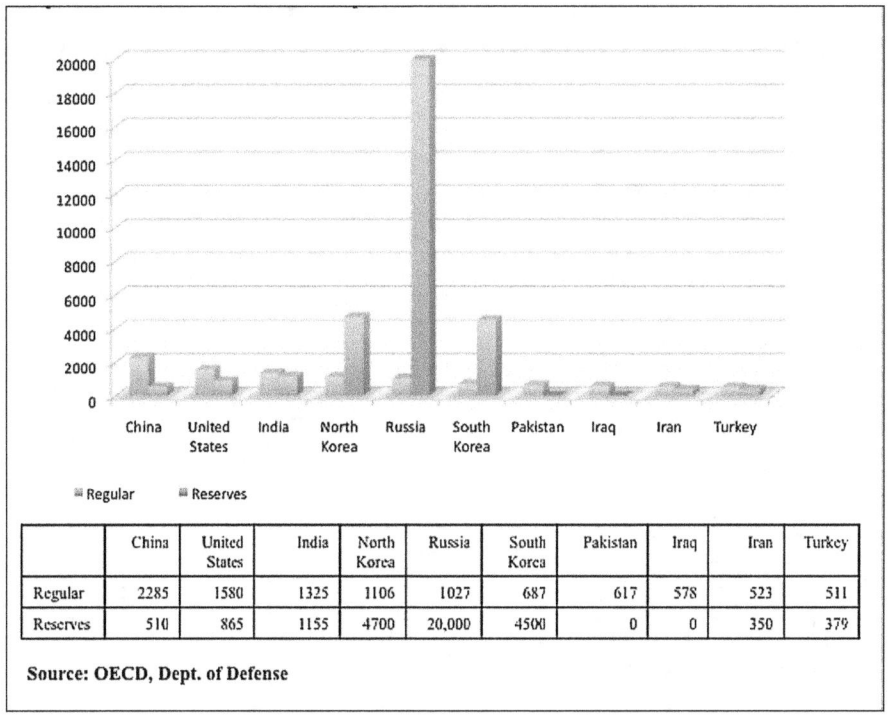

| | China | United States | India | North Korea | Russia | South Korea | Pakistan | Iraq | Iran | Turkey |
|---|---|---|---|---|---|---|---|---|---|---|
| Regular | 2285 | 1580 | 1325 | 1106 | 1027 | 687 | 617 | 578 | 523 | 511 |
| Reserves | 510 | 865 | 1155 | 4700 | 20,000 | 4500 | 0 | 0 | 350 | 379 |

**Source: OECD, Dept. of Defense**

**Fig 10 Armed forces, in 1000s of troops**

The actual monetary amounts spent were quite different due to more sophisticated and costly armaments among the different leading military nations of the world as shown in Figure 11.

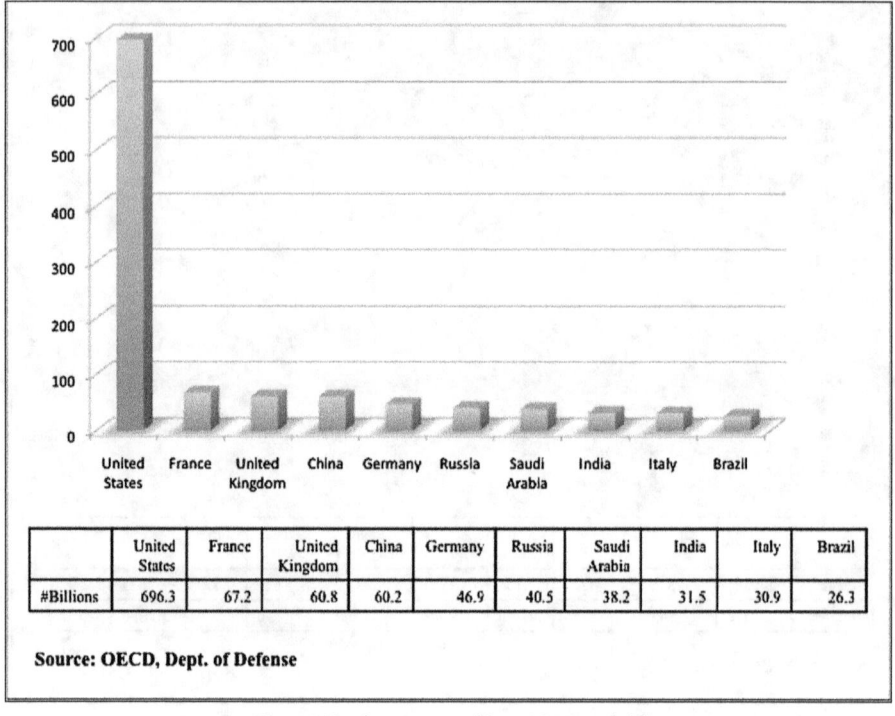

| | United States | France | United Kingdom | China | Germany | Russia | Saudi Arabia | India | Italy | Brazil |
|---|---|---|---|---|---|---|---|---|---|---|
| #Billions | 696.3 | 67.2 | 60.8 | 60.2 | 46.9 | 40.5 | 38.2 | 31.5 | 30.9 | 26.3 |

Source: OECD, Dept. of Defense

Fig 11 Defense spending 2008, # billions

These monetary expenditures reflect radically different approaches to armament philosophies and to costs of soldiers. While China has the largest armed forces in the world, it has a much lower salary basis to maintain these forces and spends considerably less on weaponry. The United States does the contrary. It spends more than any other nation both on salaries for its troops and modern weaponry.

But for purposes of economic analysis, the percentage of GDP being spent is the most important and revealing. As can be seen from Figure 12, the United States leads, not just in total dollars spent but also in the percentage of GDP spent on defense.

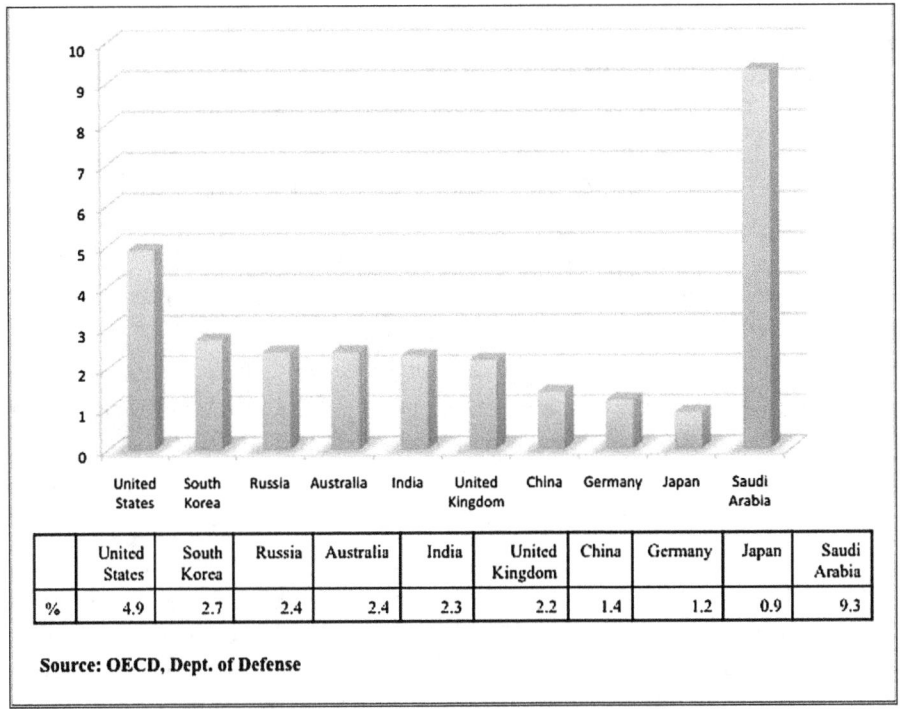

| | United States | South Korea | Russia | Australia | India | United Kingdom | China | Germany | Japan | Saudi Arabia |
|---|---|---|---|---|---|---|---|---|---|---|
| % | 4.9 | 2.7 | 2.4 | 2.4 | 2.3 | 2.2 | 1.4 | 1.2 | 0.9 | 9.3 |

Source: OECD, Dept. of Defense

Fig 12. Defense spending as % of GDP

With the exception of Saudi Arabia, which is obligated by its commercial ties with the U.S. to buy weaponry from the U.S., no other country of the leading nations has spent as much in total or as a percentage of the GDP as the United States. In fact, the above figures show that almost all other nations spent half as much of a percentage of GDP as the United States. It is probable that, if this percentage of GDP being spent for defense purposes was cut in half, the funds available to spend on alternative capital projects would increase long term GDP growth by an annualized 1 to 2 percent.

## _Changing War Characteristics_

Becoming readily apparent in Iraq, modern insurgency warfare is fought on a whole new plane. The United States rolled across Iraq with its tremendous hardware superiority. Tanks and mobile troops, along with its awesome air power, were so far superior to the fighting power of Saddam Hussein's troops that resistance was virtually non-existent. Although President Bush and Defense Secretary Donald Rumsfeld declared success almost immediately, it was also apparent that this was far from the truth. The insurgents began the real resistance with roadside bombs (IED devices). Snipers and guerrilla tactics made the occupation infinitely more difficult than the invasion. But the experts said the United States' position was to train Iraqi troops to manage their own country. With troop deaths increasing, the Pentagon came up with a new strategy - a surge of troops and an alliance with dissident Shiite Iraqis. Free elections were held and, in 2010, the United States began pulling out troops from a level of about 150,000 troops to 50,000. This presence will be much lower by mid-2012. It was declared that the Iraqis were ready to run their own country and police it with their own troops. Many experts doubted this and it remains to be seen if the new government can form the necessary coalition and keep its troops together. World opinion is still out on the verdict. Universally, it was admitted that the war began on the false premise that Saddam Hussein had weapons of mass destruction. As far as nation building, even the most hawkish of American military experts were highly doubtful that democracy could be imposed through military force. Most tellingly, almost no one could show that Al Qaeda and the 9/11 bombing of the World Trade Center were in any way related to Iraq.

Simultaneous to Iraq, the United States was fighting another insurgency war in Afghanistan. The United States is in its tenth year fighting the famous Afghanistan guerrillas. Notwithstanding the fact that these people were notorious for destroying invading armies, the U.S. felt it could do what Britain, the Soviet Union, and India had not been able to accomplish: fight these fierce tribesmen in their rugged terrain on their own grounds with their own rules. General David Petraeus, the military hero of Iraq and the foremost insurgency strategist of the United States, took over command of the U.S. troops and an Iraqi-type surge was mounted in 2010 with a deadline of September 2011 for the troops to remain. But reports were coming out of Afghanistan that, when the United States won a battle, almost immediately 150 new troops appeared to replace the defeated Taliban soldiers. Most disappointing of all was the Karzai government of Afghanistan, which most observers believe is totally corrupt and inept.

## New Anti-Insurgency Tactics

In order to economize and adapt to the new type of conflicts, the kind with insurgents fighting a guerrilla-type conflict, the United States would do well to rethink its whole approach of large troop deployment. Smaller deployments of specially trained units such as the Navy Seals or Army Rangers could be used. Instead of attacking a country with the massive troop movements as in Iraq or Afghanistan, special units could be released to do such things as kill Bin Laden, a major victory even though it occurred in Pakistan, not Afghanistan.

Of course, some conventional firepower could still be maintained but in a much smaller scale. Large bases in different parts of the world should be cut back. The development of highly expensive new airplanes and tanks should be limited. New, extremely expensive naval ships such as aircraft carriers should be frozen. Instead, lesser expensive weaponry for the special services could be developed. But overall, there should be a dependence on diplomacy, joint international peace keeping forces, and the use of the Special Forces and such things as the newly developed unmanned drones.

Britain, which usually follows the United States closely and spends an estimated 2.2 percent of its GDP on defense, has just announced, through its new conservative government under Prime Minister David Cameron, just such an approach. Britain is ranked third behind the United States and China in global defense spending with a 2009 defense budget of almost $75 billion. Its announced defense cuts were made to rein in wasteful spending and as part of an overall effort to balance its budget. In this regard, Britain is following the lead of other European nations to work toward balancing their budgets and reducing programs which they consider non-essential.

## Cost Spiral of Defense Expenditures

Manpower in all-volunteer armies, as most industrialized countries have today, is expensive. Pay has to be competitive. Moreover, in the United States of America, a big burden is the cost of health care for current and former servicemen and their families. Although Secretary of Defense Robert Gates warned of spiraling healthcare costs, before he retired, the U.S.

Congress is very generous to ex-servicemen and women with the support of a grateful citizenry.

One way to respond to spiraling manpower costs is to rely on technology. However, studies show that the price of combat planes and warships has risen faster than inflation and generally more than increases in GDP. Using his law of incremental costs for military spending, the aerospace luminary, Norman Augustine has extrapolated costs to the following absurd but startling conclusion:

> "In the year 2054, the entire defense budget of the U.S. will purchase just one aircraft. This aircraft will have to be shared by the Air Force and Navy 3.5 days per week, except for leap year, when it will be made available to the Marines for the extra day."

The rising cost of military equipment is an old curse. Philip Pugh, in a 1986 study of shipbuilding costs since the end of the Napoleonic Wars, argues that the Industrial Revolution made the problem more acute. The rapid pace of technological change set off a race to build more powerful and more heavily armed battleships. At some time as unit prices rise, one of two things must happen: countries must cut back on their ambitions or seek game-changing technology.

Pugh also identified another intriguing trend: the race for bigger and better weapons is fiercest in peacetimes but tends to fall once war actually breaks out. At that point, quantity takes precedent over quality and prices drop. This may explain, in part, why the cold war never turned hot: it was too profitable just to produce and upgrade the weaponry.

Another rule is Augustine's law of the "last 10 percent of performance generates one-third of the cost and two-thirds of the problems... Such is part of the cost spiral of modern warfare and weapon development: delay raises costs and governments postpone further work to avoid budget-busting with higher long-term costs resulting." As an example, there were supposed to be 132 Stealth B-2 bombers built by the U.S. but only 20 were built at a cost of $2 billion each.

One special area of expenditures, where the country must not cut, is on the care of our veterans when they come home. Citizens of all political persuasions claim to "support our troops." Actions and money speak louder than words and the nation owes its veterans. Rules and regulations that prevent military medics from being paramedics or military truck drivers from being commercial truck drivers without training and licensing are not just wasteful but downright stupid. If our men and women can serve a function under sniper fire or the threat of IEDs, they can serve that function here at home.

In the final analysis, what is to be the answer as to defense? Are nations going to spend an increasingly high amount of money on modern weaponry and numerous troops or is there going to be some attempt at downsizing or what some call disarmament? But, most importantly, as is the theme of this work, decisions have to be made as to just what is necessary in the defense of a country, what is affordable, and what is the public willing to spend in an era of realization that all resources are limited. But maybe, especially limited is the amount of money federal governments really have to spend and which the public is willing to pay through the price of higher taxes.

## Strategy or Armament

Andres Krepinevich, director of the Washington think tank, Centre for Strategic and Budgetary Assessment, has argued that America is at a crossroads similar to that of Great Britain at the turn of the 20th century when it faced a rising America, an expansionist Russia, and a quickly industrializing Germany and Japan. Britain's choice was to make a series of concessions. It surrendered Latin America to the U.S., supported Japan to check Russia, and made up with France to confront Germany. As he said so succinctly, "Strategy is what you need when you don't have any more money." He went on in this line, "Britain was a declining power but it managed to hang on for quite a long time with intelligent strategy."

There are many things the United States can do at this juncture. But, the first thing is to realize that it can't continue to spend the amount of money and percentage of GDP that it is presently spending on defense. The beginning of a sound policy today might be for America to withdraw from its costly and unwinnable war in Afghanistan, to pull out troops in Europe and to cut back on conventional troop maintenance. The fear might be that, in doing these things, America may be perceived as becoming weak and a target to its enemies. But a careful analysis should show, even with significant and well-planned reductions, American will still maintain the biggest profile in military terms in the world. And as with Great Britain, strategy and diplomacy may more than make up for cost reductions. Sound management and living within budgetary means should never be conceived as weakness in national defense.

## Present Debate on Budgetary Adjustment

In the hotly debated federal budget for FY 2010 and 2011, there was much talk of cutting all and every discretionary account except for defense. Former Secretary of Defense Gates proposed a slight increase of 5 percent for FY 2010 but, nevertheless, it was an increase. Gates emphasized to his command staff that budgetary cuts will come but that it would be far better to anticipate them and control them from a military point of view rather than letting the politicians make arbitrary cuts. In line with this thinking was Gates' mandate to tighten up bid procedures, taking out much of the slack presently in the system. Hopefully, this will begin to eliminate such wasteful spending as $600 screwdrivers and $1000 toilet seats. Also observations have been made that procedures and scope of fixed price contracts, which traditionally had costly overrides, must be reviewed. Even by most defense experts' admission, much of traditional bidding has been "low ball" in order to win contracts that then had costly overrides to bring the contracts to completion.

There has been some talk of suspension of what are considered useless new weaponry system such as a proposed marine amphibious landing craft.

But even with all these cuts the cost of America's defense is projected to continue to increase in the coming years. Secretary of Defense Leon Panetta has argued that cuts in excess of $40 billion annually will seriously harm the United States of America's Defenses.

Deep and concerted analysis must be made for really big defense changes including the closing of bases, especially overseas bases and a general downsizing and serious consideration to committing to other costly wars. In other words, America's very posture as the world's policeman must be rethought.

# CHAPTER VI

# SOCIAL SECURITY

The New Head
of
$ocial $ecurity

*"The day must come when the nation's whole scale of living must be reduced. If that day comes, parliament must lay the burden equally on all classes."*

WINSTON CHURCHILL

*"Capitals are increased by parsimony and decreased by prodigality and misconduct. By what a frugal man saves annually he not only affords maintenance to an additional number of hands – but – he establishes as it were a perpetual fund for the maintenance of an equal number in all times to come."*

ADAM SMITH

*"Let me assert my belief that the only thing we have to fear is fear itself – nameless, unreasoning, unjustified terror that paralyses needed effort to convert retreat into advance."*

FRANKLIN D. ROOSEVELT

In 1918, Charles Ponzi sold people in Brooklyn, New York on the idea that, if they gave him money, he would invest it in postal service financial instruments and it would return them 10 percent interest. It was an attractive idea, for Mr. Ponzi represented it as a guaranteed return. Investors flocked to give Ponzi money but there was one problem: Ponzi was returning these attractive dividends by bringing in new money. In other words, rather than shrewd investing, Ponzi was using other people's money to pay current dividends. The scheme was successful at first but, as it grew bigger, problems developed. There wasn't enough new money to keep up with the dividends Ponzi promised. A panic ensued and the police were called in. Ponzi was arrested and the press latched on to the scandalous story of what became known as a "Ponzi scheme." Unfortunately, many poor people, who really couldn't afford to lose, lost everything.

Over the years, many similar schemes were developed in America in different locations and with other types of investments. They were all called Ponzi schemes because they promised guaranteed returns but only made those returns out of new money coming in without investing money in anything.

The latest such venture that got wide public attention was promoted by an investment czar out of New York named Bernie Madoff. He promised investors sweet returns of at least 12 percent annually. At first, based on his investing acumen, Madoff was able to pay these returns. But, when investments were short in what they were yielding, Madoff began to dip into his pool of money, into the principal. Madoff himself has stated, "It just started with me covering a short position. We had so much cash in the banks and it was so simple. I controlled everything, even the accounting audits." It is noteworthy that Madoff ran this scheme for 20 years and had over $65 billion in account value. Thousands of people, both small and large investors, very wealthy and middle class people, invested. They even begged

Madoff to take their money. The sad part was that the investment business Madoff ran started out in a very legitimate way and Madoff held the claim to being a skilled investment adviser. When the financial markets began their collapse in 2008, investors were afraid. And in their fear, they began massive withdrawals from Madoff. These withdrawals were the cause of the discovery of what Madoff was actually running.

Ponzi was successful because he promised a panacea: a guaranteed, decent return. It was packaged and sold by a man who was well-presented and highly believable. Madoff ran his operations for many years and had people, from all over, from every strata of society, give him money to invest. He presented a coherent scheme. He looked the part of a successful operator, distinguished, well-spoken, and with a personality that immediately had people liking him. His investors were given a product which sounded good - not too good - but steady with guaranteed returns. [In the interest of full disclosure, one of the co-authors of the book, Albert Parish, pled guilty to securities fraud based on investing money in other ways than requested by investors without informing investors.]

In 1934, President Roosevelt presented an idea to the American public of a guaranteed steady return of money to them for their retirement. He proposed to establish a fund run by the government of the United States that would supplement people's income for their retirement. After coming out of the Great Depression, where individuals lost everything, it was met with almost instant public approval. People wanted to believe. They wanted something that would give them some security. The idea was simple. All Americans would pay into the new Social Security fund (actually named OASDI - Old Age Survivor and Disability Insurance) and at a certain age, up to the time they died, Americans would be paid a monthly stipend. At the time of its initiation, the American population had a certain composition with a high percentage of people working and paying into Social Security. The longevity of the average American was such that, if people retired at 65, they would be expected to live and receive these guaranteed monthly Social Security payments for, at most, only 5 years. The actuarial mathematics worked in favor of the government being able to meet its payments out of current income. During the first 40 years, a surplus was developed in this Social Security Trust Fund. But, where was the trust fund money kept? Since it was run by the American government, it all went into the general fund and I.O.U.'s were issued. In other words, there was a filing cabinet and later an electronic entry system, noting that so much money accumulated in the trust fund.

As long as more money was coming in than that promised people in retirement, everything was fine, much like the Ponzi or Madoff schemes. The fact is that, if the government wasn't running Social Security, it would have been deemed a Ponzi scheme and the people running it would have been indicted.

By the 1980's, the population of the United States had so changed that a fix was required in the system. Retirement ages were raised and the taxes charged to the working men and women were increased. But the specter of a broken system persisted and the talk again was for changing the parameters of the system, either this or it would bankrupt the country.

Through the 75-plus years of Social Security, a surplus of $2.7 trillion went into the U.S. Treasury. However with an ever greater number of older Americans in retirement versus younger Americans paying the Social Security taxes, due to the Great Recession in 2010, the system was once again in deficit and talk was, by 2035, it would be unsustainable. Where will the money to pay the deficit come from? Since it is considered an entitlement, i.e. an obligation of the United States' government, it will have to come from the general budget, a budget which already is deep in the red. The concept of Social Security is now embedded as a right of Americans, a birthright. But is it really? Up to the present, Americans have believed that federal spending for certain things to maintain a certain standard of living was an American social guarantee.

To demonstrate how Social Security works, let's take the example of Chris Brown, a 40 year old with a blue-collar job on an assembly line at Robb Steel Inc. Chris earns $40,000 per year in wages. He also receives benefits like health insurance, group life insurance, etc. For his retirement planning, Chris saves 6.20 percent of his salary or $2,480 per year. Robb Steel, Inc. matches his savings so another $2,480 is added to Chris' account.

Now, suppose that Robb Steel were to use some of Chris' money for its operating expenses and to pay interest on corporate debt. The rest of Chris' money is used to pay the retirement benefits of existing retirees of Robb Steel Inc. since the company has borrowed its entire savings and has no funds to pay these retirees otherwise. So, each year, Robb Steel does two things. First, it issues an I.O.U. to Chris' retirement account. This year, for example, Chris' account would get an I.O.U. of $4,960. Second, each year, Robb Steel Inc. sends Chris a statement showing how much money he has earned in each year he worked for the company and an estimate of how much he will receive at retirement, at age 65.

What would happen if Robb Steel Inc. were audited? Obviously, it would be charged with fraud and its financial executives sent to prison for operating a so-called Ponzi scheme. As described above, a Ponzi scheme is exactly what Robb Steel was running, i.e. a criminal venture in which savings of current investors like Chris have their money used to pay prior investors and to pay expenses of the scheme's perpetuators. In such an enterprise, no investments are made with the savings.

However, if the name Robb Steel Company is changed to OASDI, there is no crime. For this is Social Security and, since it is the United States government, it is legal. Unfortunately, this description of Robb Steel Inc.'s actions perfectly matches what happens in today's Social Security system. The employee saves 6.2 percent of his wages, up to the current $106,800 cap, and his employer matches that amount. Social Security then uses most of the funds coming in to pay benefits to current retirees and borrows the rest that might be needed to pay such retirees. I.O.U's are issued to the current working people who are paying into the system and each year an estimate of benefits is mailed to them even though there are no investments, only I.O.U.'s to back the estimate of benefits accruing.

As of Dec. 31, 2009, the estimated liability (the I.O.U.'s issued to the current savers) was for about $18 trillion. That's $18,000,000,000,000 or roughly $58,000 for every man, women, and child in the U.S. This is about 40 percent greater than the GDP of the United States for a full year or, in other words, 40 percent greater than the total U.S. economy. As with so much in the present federal government, there is a serious difference in what the public perceives the government is spending and committing to and what is actually being spent and obligated.

Things are getting worse. The payroll tax cut of 2011-2012 reduced the percentage paid to Social Security by the worker to 4.2% from 6.2%. On an average $50,000 household income, this 2% cut will result in a $1,000 per year reduction, or around $40 bi-weekly paycheck. But this cut takes 16% from Social Security taxes bringing the day of insolvency closer.

There was nothing wrong with the public retirement system developed in 1934. It was created as a system to supplement retirement, as a supplement to private source retirement. It was never conceived of in its initiation to be the primary, much less the sole, source of the average American's retirement income. Furthermore, Social Security was structured as intergenerational where the next generation of workers would fund the retirement benefits of the prior generation. Such a plan could only work under three assumptions: 1) that generations are of approximately the same size so that the ratio of workers paying into the system to retirees drawing benefits remains stable, 2) that human life spans would be constant so the number of years the average retiree receives benefits remains stable, and 3) that any taxes paid into the system in excess of benefits paid out are invested for the benefit of retirees in the future. Unfortunately, there has not been the proper adjustment for the dramatic changing of all of these conditions.

As of 2009, the total being paid out slightly exceeded the total coming in. The difference should have been made up from the accumulated surpluses from prior years. However, since these surpluses were only I.O.U.s, the federal government had to pay this difference from general funds. Since the federal government was in deficit, these obligations were paid through the government borrowing these funds from others, the Chinese for example. Several times in the 75 year operation of Social Security, when shortfalls in funding were recognized, adjustments to retirement age and taxes being paid were made. This undoubtedly will be done again.

In the second Bush administration, there was an attempt to privatize Social Security, to allow individuals to make their own investment decisions as to what they would do with the funds they were saving instead of just getting I.O.U's. The attempt failed miserably. Present retirees feared they would be cut off from their retirement monies. Most importantly, there was no proof that retirement systems as big as the American Social Security system could be privately run. The example of Chile was given as a country with a successful private Social Security system, however Chile is a very small compared to the size of the American economic system and population.

Of course, this effort of privatization only focused on one of the defects of the present system, that of investing the surplus funds. A more important question is how Social Security will be funded as part of the social overhead of the United States. As pointed out throughout this book, the United States is at a point where it must analyze and decide on basic structural changes required in the economy or make decisions of design for it to remain a viable entity. If such changes are not made voluntarily, in a planned manner, the markets will force such changes and the way the changes are made while their results will probably not be what the American public wants. In this context, the United States will have to make radical changes to its public support system for many things including its system of retirement of older Americans from the work force.

## Social Security – Some Solutions

Decisions have to be made concerning Social Security in America. As it presently stands its viability is questionable. To solve the Social Security deficit, there are various solutions. One would be to increase revenue coming into the system. There are several ways this can be done. Increase the 6.2 percent tax rate on wages that both employee and employer pay. Currently, employees pay 4.2%, not 6.2%. When that rate goes back up (and it will mean a 48% hike in the tax paid by the employees) arguments will undoubtedly ensue. It probably would be easier to raise the rate beyond 6.2% at that time rather than re-visiting the issue later. Many workers presently pay more in this tax than they do in income taxes and this option would especially affect the low-income workers proportionately more than the higher income workers. Such a change would be the broadest change of all the solutions. A second way would be to raise the amount of wages on which the tax applies. Presently, it is at $106,800 although that limit is raised each year, adjusted for inflation. A third way would be to broaden the income on which the tax applies to include such non-wage income like interest, dividends, capital gains, benefits, etc. The Affordable Health Care Act of 2010 applied the Medicare tax to additional kinds of income, as an example of how this might work. Fourth, the population that pays the tax increases. This implies that more workers, including immigrants, pay into the system. It also implies there will be more beneficiaries further down the road. So, in essence, it is only a temporary help. Finally, within this solution would be an increase of wage growth so workers make more income and can pay more in payroll taxes. This, of course, carries the greatest overall economic benefit but will ultimately turn on higher productivity which in turn will require greater skills, knowledge, and education, and greater capital investment.

The second solution is to decrease Social Security expenditures. There would be several ways of doing this. First, there could be a decrease in monthly benefits to existing and/or future retirees. A reduction of 7 percent to current beneficiaries would solve the Social Security deficit problem for many years. Another way of doing this would be to decrease the growth rate in benefits. For 2010 and 2011, the rate was set at 0 percent due to very low inflation. But tying the growth rate to an index that rises less, on average, than wages could be one way of doing this. Another would be means-testing benefits so that, as income in retirement rises, benefits decrease. Under this approach, all retirees would still actually receive at least what they paid in OADSI taxes. Finally, there could be an increase in the retirement age to 70 years old for all workers above a current age of, let's say, 45 years old. This would adjust the average life span covered. Of course, average life spans vary by race, gender, and income, so such a change does not affect everyone equally (hence the term "average lifespan").

The third solution, and most controversial, is to drop Social Security altogether. Such a solution would entail paying off existing and soon-to-be retirees over a period of 30 years or so. If this were done all at once, the cost would be a staggering $18 trillion by some estimates. With this approach, the OASDI tax would go away and workers would save for retirement in IRA or 401-K type accounts. This would result in almost $1 trillion annually in private savings which, in turn, would create significant changes in stock and capital markets given the size of the United States. The nation of Chile undertook such an option under the guidance of the Chicago School of monetarists and even then, with a comparatively small economy, it was a difficult transition.

All of these solutions have economic, social, and demographic considerations and problems. And most obviously, and perhaps ominously, all have political considerations to deal with. Some of these considerations make one or another approach a non-starter but doing nothing in itself, given the arithmetic of the current system of Social Security, is the biggest non-starter of all.

A method of satisfying the social overhead of older Americans, who have worked all their lives and earned the right to a retirement during their last years, must be found. The current system cannot be maintained and almost definitely will result in a disaster if not modified in some manner.

# CHAPTER VII

# UNEMPLOYMENT

*"The outstanding faults of the economic society in which we live are its failure to provide for full employment, and its arbitrary and inequitable distribution of wealth and income."*

JOHN MAYNARD KEYNES

*"The community lacks goods and a good million and a quarter people lack work. It is certainly one of the highest functions of national finance and credit to bridge the gap b/w the two."*

WINSTON CHURCHILL

*"I tell you: one must have chaos in one, to give birth to a dancing star."*

FRIEDRICH NIETZSCHE

*"Remember, there is no success without hard work."*

SOPHOCLES

During the Great Recession of 2007-10, the major economic problem was unemployment. Not since the Great Depression of 1929-32, with its 25 percent unemployment level, have so many Americans, both as a percentage of the work force and in total number, been unemployed. America has always prided itself on being a country where work was abundant for those seeking it. America welcomed those "huddled and poor immigrants" to fill those low-paying but necessary jobs that no one else wanted. There was a job for everyone who was willing and able to work.

But in this recession, America faced something prevalent in Europe but totally new in America - a high rate of unemployment which risks becoming permanent. This problem of so many jobless creates a myriad of problems, both sociological and political.

During past recessions, Americans thought "this time it is different" and usually it wasn't. This present situation comes with two major differences from America's past: a weakened education system combined with a vastly changing technological world that requires an educated workforce. This twin, good-bad situation will continue to cause great disruptions in America's economy and no simple political fixes, contrary to what many politicians are saying, will solve it in the near term. It will take years and a complete systemic change to correct the structural imbalances.

With the United States in the leadership position, the world has made great technological progress in the past 20 years with computers finally beginning to realize their potential as predicted at their birth in mid-20th century. Computers advanced from scientific equipment used to number-crunch to commodities used by everyone, including children and virtually every American household. As Moore's law kicked in, increased capacities grew exponentially with lower costs for increased computing power. "Wintel," a combination of microchips from Intel with a universal operating system from Microsoft, became the standard and brought the PC (personal computer) to the masses. Coupled with the virtual connectivity and information sharing of the internet, the current generation is witnessing a new economic revolution maybe even greater, and possibly even more socially disruptive, than the original Industrial Revolution that began in the 19th Century.

In most economic textbooks, "capital" and "labor" are considered substitutes for one another. Of course, in the real world, capital and labor serve as both substitutes and complements to production and can be so at the same time. Traditionally, capital and technology are fixed inputs to production while labor is a variable input. However, this is becoming less true in modern economies. The advancement of technology necessitates upgrading more frequently, so that the firm may remain competitive while varying labor input. This is often accomplished by laying off workers, resulting in higher turnover costs and an elongated learning curve faced by rehired or new workers.

The most important overall economic measure of labor is unit labor costs. It measures the dollar cost of labor per unit of output produced. It is also a calculation of the ratio of wages, which measure the dollar cost of labor per man-hour worked to average product, which measures the output produced per man-hour worked. A firm can reduce unit labor costs in its efforts to maximize profits by reducing wages or raising average product. Unfortunately for all concerned, reducing wages leads to uncertain and unhappy workers which in turn, can reduce productivity. It has been shown in many studies that "happy" workers are more productive workers. Still, many firms cut wages to compete with other firms. Another way of compensating is to reduce hours worked or to impose furloughs to avoid cutting wages, although the net effect is the same, lower take-home pay for the workers. Employers using these techniques hope productivity does not suffer as much as with directly cutting wages.

One of the most common ways of boosting productivity to remain competitive is through capital expenditures for new equipment and technology. From this alternative, there is higher productivity that may also reduce total man hours of labor for a given level of required output or boosts output with the same amount of labor. Capital expenditures serve simultaneously as both a substitute and complement to labor. Of course, the new equipment and technology will come at a cost of a learning curve, sacrificing some productivity at least in the short term. The smart firm determines its levels of capital and labor used in production for any level of output by using both until the ratios of marginal products to cost per hour of labor and capital are equal. With the rapid pace of technological progress, the levels of employment of capital and labor change more frequently than in the past as the firm moves more rapidly along the least cost expansion path described by these equal ratios.

As employees are faced with learning curves, uncertainty rises among them. This uncertainty is based on the assumption that "human capital" depreciates just like physical capital and technology. Of course, human capital depreciation comes in various forms. People get older and less able to do the same physical work. People may also become physically sick and unable to do any work. Skills also become "rusty" and even obsolete because of lack of use or technology's substitution. While people cannot control the age factor, they can mitigate sickness by entering preventive health programs, eating properly, ceasing smoking, and engaging in exercise.

As physical capital depreciates, firms undertake replacement investment. As human capital depreciates, replacement investment can also be undertaken through continuing education and retraining. This can give a boost, allowing for a shorter and flatter learning curve. The ability and programming to allow workers to acquire new skills are vitally important in a technologically progressing society. While some workers are uncertain, or even downright afraid of structural change, it must be accepted and promoted in order for a society to remain productive. In the coal mines of West Virginia in the 1930's, the labor leader, John L. Lewis, worked with management to introduce new technology. While it reduced some jobs, it had a two-fold positive result: it made coal mining safer for the worker and allowed the companies to remain competitive with alternate fuel sources.

During the Great Recession of 2007-10, workers experienced a longer period of unemployment on average than anything in 80 years. The group called the "99-ers," those who have been out of work for more than 99 weeks and out of unemployment insurance is growing. They represent the tip of the iceberg of those who are suffering from structural unemployment.

Some employers refuse to even consider hiring the long-term unemployed, fearing that this group's productivity will be lower as their skills have not been recently used. The longer the time a person is unemployed, the tougher it is to find a job. Thus long-term unemployment becomes a self-fulfilling prophesy. The longer a person is not employed, the more probable it becomes that he/she never re-enters the employment market.

It is absolutely essential for economic well-being and indeed for the country's long-term economic survival as the world's leading economic power to understand these concepts of changing the job structure. Educational reform that gets the unemployed retrained in the short term and prepares the next generation to function in a new world of ever-changing technology is crucial. The young generally accept new ideas faster than the old because they are more flexible and can adjust faster. We just have to look at older people and their acceptance of systems such as emails compared to the young, who are complaining that email is way too slow and that the use of texting and social networking is far better. The lesson is simple: firms and workers must adjust to the new methods of networking and marketing, to new methods of manufacturing and outsourcing. It is simply no longer a matter of cheaper-labor countries out-manufacturing the United States. Just as what occurred with Japanese products at the end of World War II, the labor cost differential disappears quickly and, instead, better manufacturing, better technology, and simply more imaginative product development and marketing end up leaving the new economies with a permanent advantage.

The assimilation of technology by economic participants will continue. To use a Star Trek phrase, "resistance is futile." This means that work lives will be dramatically changed and not just for the short term but for the long term. America is waking up to the fact that the unemployment developed out of the 2007-10 contraction will not simply disappear. Politicians are speaking of bringing down an unemployment rate of about 8 percent that has stubbornly refused to move lower quicker. The times when a person would graduate from high school, go to work for an automobile or steel company, spend the next 40 years there with comfortable middle class wages, a defined benefit retirement program, a house paid off in 30 years of employment at the same factory or business, children raised and educated in suburbia who go on to exceed the economic levels of their parents have largely disappeared. In the new paradigm, in the new America, in the new economic era, the average American worker will have a half dozen or more careers over his or her lifetime. He or she will have been retrained any number of times to stay current with new technology. Thus, the new American worker will have to be constantly updating his or her work skills. Old skills will be discarded and new ones acquired constantly. Most tellingly, as is happening in the quickest developing economies of this new century, in China and India, in Brazil and Mexico, labor retraining will have to be matched by labor mobility. Labor will have to train for jobs and be willing to move to where the jobs are located. This will have far reaching consequences both economically and politically. The only question will be how rapidly America will adapt, not whether America will or won't adapt.

## Structural Unemployment

There is much talk of the high employment rates which have plagued America since the Great Recession of 2007-10. Fingers have been pointed and political accusations have been made of both the Bush and Obama administrations. But, what has not been brought to the American public's attention is that these high rates of unemployment are really a product of structural changes, not necessarily or even primarily the result of inept political decisions.

The problems with America's educational system, discussed in other parts of this book, are undoubtedly a principle factor in such high unemployment rates. However, of equal or even greater importance are the economic realities of a new world economic system, the consequences of what is called globalization. This is a systematic cause of shifts in employment and has been both promoted and embraced by America. It involves shifting manufacturing and economic activity to areas under the comparative advantage doctrine. Low wages, skill sets of workers, and a series of other economic and developmental aspects enter into the equation in globalization. It is also the modus operandi under globalization that multinational companies, such as those common in all developed countries and which are prominent in the United States, thrive on such operations. A company such as Dell Computer can have manufacturing operations in any number of countries for any number of components that go into their computers and have design, sales, distribution, warehousing, and administrative functions in any number of countries. Dell can take an order in the United States and immediately place orders for different components of the computer being produced in a dozen other countries with shipment and assembly occurring in yet another country and sales and distribution occurring in yet another country. The driving force is economics, where it's cheapest and best to accomplish the functions.

The biggest consumer goods distribution company in the world, the quintessentially American company, Wal-Mart is the perfect example. Wal-Mart buys products from companies all over the world on an automatic reorder re-inventory system. To maintain its exceptionally cheap products, it now purchases more of the items they sell from outside the United States than within.

Two vivid examples of recent developments will illustrate the effects of this activity. They are examples where globalization is benefitting the United States in much cheaper and better quality goods but is costing the United States the benefits of jobs that would normally be American based. They are in very different sectors of the economy, one in infrastructure and one in consumer goods. The first concerns a technological product, an area in which the United States has been and still remains the world leader. It is the I-Pad produced by Apple. Apple, with its normal astute development, came up with a new I-Pad, which has many advanced features that other such products released before it did not possess. Thus, an archtypical American technological company did what the United States excels at: it developed technology that led the market and did it in the context of an American company. This was true of the technicians who performed the R&D work, true of the top management and even of the marketing people but sadly was not true of the actual production of I-Pads. For this, Apple executives went to the Chinese. A whole new city was constructed in China. Chinese workers were recruited, trained, and paid $400 monthly to build the I-Pads. They were housed in special dormitories, ate at special company mess halls and, were extremely cost effective. So the American product marketed by Apple was in fact producing many new jobs, but the majority in China.

The second example is even more startling. It involves the rebuilding of American infrastructure. In San Francisco, the Oakland Bay Bridge was damaged by an earthquake and needed either major repairs or had to be replaced. This is, in fact, a very common occurrence in America. Much infrastructure is old, has been neglected, and needs replacement. Traditionally, such work produced one hundred percent American jobs. After all, it requires extensive on-site manual labor. However, a strange thing happened. San Francisco decided it was not going to take federal government money with the "buy America" provisions such aid specified. Instead, it put the project out for international bid. A strange arrangement was made with a consortium of American Bridge and Fluor Enterprises being a the primary contractors, doing all the on-site labor, but with a Chinese company Shanghai Zhenhua Heavy Industries located in Shanghai providing the fabrication of the massive spans of steel (half a football field in length). The total cost of the project was to be $7.2 billion and, by subcontracting the fabrication work, a total of $400 million was saved over American fabrication. There was even some question if any American fabrication company could handle a job of this magnitude. There are now 3,000 workers in China working to produce the 28 bridge decks for the 2.2 mile span. Some 250 American consultants are permanently in China to supervise the fabrication but the U.S. lost the 3,000 jobs. A typical Chinese worker on the project works from 7 a.m. to 11 p.m. and is paid $12 per day, an increase from the $9 paid previously. In both these projects, globalization prevented the formation of American jobs for American products produced by American companies. And this inexcusable loss of infrastructure jobs is not limited to this example. In New York, Chinese companies have been awarded contracts to renovate the New York City subway system and to rebuild the Alexander Hamilton Bridge in Harlem. All of these projects are public works but are financed by tolls so do not require federal funding.

In the case of consumer goods as described, the American public is assuaged by the cheaper prices of final goods resulting from the cheaper and more favorable foreign labor. For capital goods, such as infrastructure as described, the local government involved gets considerably cheaper, labor-intensive fabrication and thus saves on overall price and in some sense even in being able to do the project. So American are in a conundrum. They enjoy the cheaper prices of globalization but do they really understand the price of lost or misplaced jobs.

For politicians it becomes an almost insoluble short-term problem. They have the pressure of the present high structural unemployment that requires political reactions short term, but that may be unrealistic long term. There are few major corporations who are bucking the higher profits that result from outsourcing most of the front end production of products to cheaper labor countries. And, few Americans complain about cheaper priced consumer goods coming from China. Yet unemployment is a major political concern.

## A German Solution to High Cost Labor

Germany has faced the globalization problems of high cost labor and structural unemployment in an interesting way. They have combined government, labor, and business to keep Germany competitive in the world market, even against the cheap labor of China and India. Labor costs in Germany exceeds that of the United States, especially for qualified, higher skilled labor. What Germany has done is threefold: 1) it has reached agreement with labor to cut work weeks to lower unemployment, 2) it has worked at training its labor so it is second to none in the higher skilled labor market, and 3) the government has fomented diversification of small and medium sized capital goods industries across the whole of Germany. The result is that the high end capital goods export industry is flourishing in Germany which has become a world leader in this sector. The German economy thus has a lower structural unemployment rate than most other developed nations. German workers have shorter work weeks than in most other developed countries and have accepted these shorter weeks and reduced pay. However German worker productivity continues to be among the highest in the world.

## Present Situation

By the end of calendar year 2011, unemployment stabilized at around 8.3 percent. Projections were that it would take between 5 and 7 years to get back the jobs lost during the Great Recession. With America's population growth, there has to be a continuous production of jobs just to keep the unemployment rate even. Almost everyone believes America must create most of its jobs in technological sectors like healthcare and computers, not in traditional consumer products manufacturing and services even though manufacturing has been doing comparatively well in the recovery. But for the creation of technological jobs, America will need to have the trained workers required to perform these tasks. Without a serious revision of its educational system, this will be difficult-to-impossible to do. The United States must bring the quality of its primary and secondary school systems up significantly.

Without the "feedstock" of high school graduates, America's excellent university system cannot produce the technicians the economy needs. Without this skilled labor pool, enterprises America must have in the technological sector will not be created. The present unemployment in America is structural rather than cyclical. America cannot expect traditional businesses to fully rehire employees to fill the positions vacated during the Great Recession. Without the trained workforce to man new technological jobs, America will continue to have high levels of unemployment and workers with stagnant incomes.

# CHAPTER VIII

# HEALTH CARE

*"If the fence is strong enough, I'll sit on it."*

CYRIL SMITH

*"A right is not what somewhat gives to you, it's what no one can take away from you."*

RAMSEY CLARK

*"If only I had known, I would have become a watchmaker."*

ALBERT EINSTEIN

The most difficult, if not intractable, part of the federal, and state budget is health care costs. Medicaid expenses now consume almost half of budgets in some states and are more than one quarter of such budgets in most. Under health insurance reform, an additional 16 million people could be added to Medicaid rolls by 2014. Medicare and Medicaid alone are about 5 percent of GDP and total health care spending is about 20 percent of GDP. As the U.S. population continues to age and the average lifespan continues to rise, these percentages will also rise.

The question in modern society is what health care does the country wish to provide to its citizens and how will it be paid for? In most developed nations, health care provision is universal. In many of these nations, it has been nationalized, provided by the central government. In the United States, the system that has evolved is hodgepodge. A national program of medical care has evolved for both the elderly and for the poor (Medicare and Medicaid). There are also some state-based programs. But health insurance has been largely private which means there has been a large pool of uninsured people in America (by some estimates as many as 40 million). Up to 2010, the country had largely opposed any rational, national plan. With great consternation and opposition from the Republican Party, the Democrats under President Obama passed the first major health care reform in almost 50 years. This health care reform passed in 2010 was dubbed "Obamacare" but, in reality, was not health care reform at all. It was really health insurance reform.

For FY 2011, the projected federal spending on health care is $572 billion for Medicare and $274 billion for Medicaid. Figure 13 shows the growth of spending on these programs.

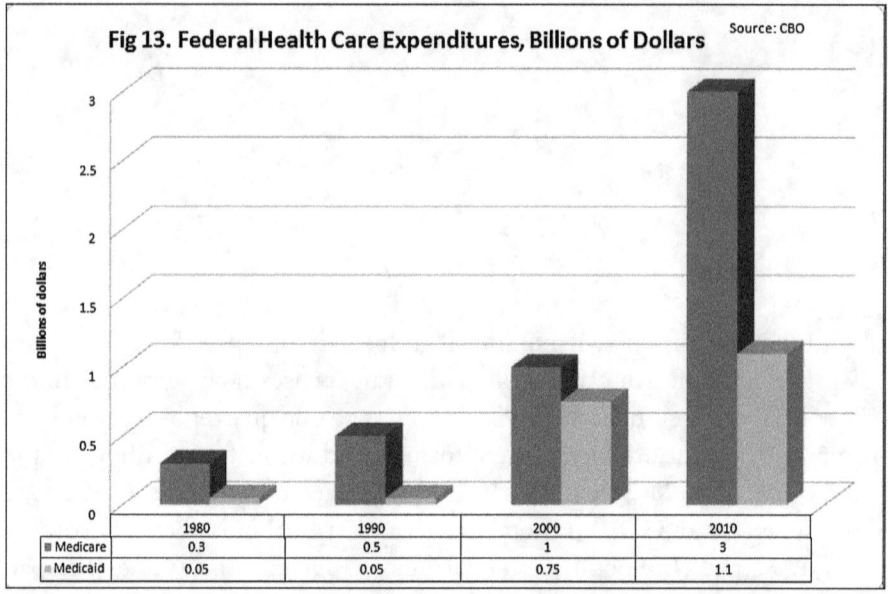

Fig 13. Federal Health Care Expenditures, Billions of Dollars    Source: CBO

| | 1980 | 1990 | 2000 | 2010 |
|---|---|---|---|---|
| Medicare | 0.3 | 0.5 | 1 | 3 |
| Medicaid | 0.05 | 0.05 | 0.75 | 1.1 |

The Affordable Health Care Act was 2,200 pages but the greatest changes were: 1) the prohibition on denying coverage for pre-existing conditions, and 2) the requirement that everyone obtain health insurance coverage – the so-called universal individual mandate. Both changes will only go into effect in 2014. As of the writing of this book, three federal judges have upheld the individual mandate and two have held it unconstitutional. The Supreme Court will have the deciding voice as to its constitutionality. If the individual mandate is thrown out, Obamacare will die, at least in its current form. Without premiums from healthy, younger people, the remaining pool of premium payers will be insufficient for companies to insure sicker people or older people with pre-existing conditions. Without a mandate, the correct logic is that healthy people will simply wait until they get sick or are injured to buy insurance, especially if pre-existing conditions are covered. Most low-income individuals will satisfy the mandate through Medicaid but many lower, and middle-income earners will receive subsidies from the federal government to pay for the insurance. Also, a factor that must be understood is that, in the current system, hospital emergency rooms must provide coverage for people without insurance. In actuality, this is what amounts to universal, subsidized health care through this system. Hospitals must charge paying or insured patients more to subsidize the people who have no insurance. What has developed then is a system in which costs are higher because many uninsured people only avail themselves of health care when there is an emergency. Preventative or on-going care is not available for those uninsured in the present system. Therefore, whether it is wanted or not, a system which is both less efficient and more costly has developed, because of the present system of voluntary insurance.

Whether the individual mandate is upheld or not, the United States must still face the economic problems of rapidly rising health care costs. Simply put, the trajectory of current costs is not financially sustainable, especially for state budgets. This raises the basic question of whether health care is a fundamental right or an economic good available only to those who can afford it. In the United States, a policy has developed which actually is a combination of the two points of view. Certain health care is viewed as a right. Emergency care for a heart attack or stroke victim, for tending to a broken leg, or to help car crash victims are examples of health care that is provided regardless of how it is paid for. Other care such as a tummy tuck, a chiropractic back adjustment, or teaching a class nutrition is clearly not health care items that are supplied regardless of the ability-to-pay either through insurance or directly. Just about everyone will agree that certain emergency care should be universal but that other so called "Cadillac coverage" should not. However, there is a huge gap in between the two extremes.

Is health care for childbirth, for flu vaccines, for cancer treatment, or for diabetes a right? And what about the prescription drugs that go along with these treatments? If a new cure develops for a previously incurable disease, should it be available only for those who have the resources - either personal wealth or insurance? Should a person with end-stage-kidney disease have dialysis withheld if he or she doesn't have the funds or means to pay for it? How about a liver, heart, kidney, or other organ transplant? Should such life saving care only be available for those of means? As another example, would an angioplasty and stent for heart disease be a right while a heart transplant is a luxury? Would it matter if the patient earned $40,000 or $250,000 a year? From a purely economic perspective, society should fund the costs of care for a patient if the patient has a sufficiently high probability of providing benefits to society to cover the cost over his remaining life. Under this standard, a 40 year old earning $250,000 a year gets the heart transplant but an 80 year old drawing $40,000 per year in retirement doesn't. Is that outcome "moral" or "fair?" Is the United States willing to provide health care universally, including to those who can't pay for it themselves? Is such health care a right for the entire lifetime of a citizen? And most importantly, who pays for it and how?

Then comes the question that is central and not spoken of, namely if the country is forced to ration care more than is does presently, who decides who gets what and when? Make no mistake about it, health care is rationed now. Insurance companies, and even doctors to a lesser extent, decide who gets what care unless the patient is wealthy enough to write his own check for it. And then, with some procedures, such as organ transplants, even those patients who can write a check can't always legally get the organ such as a liver or kidney. More and more, world citizens of developed nations are looking to lesser developed countries for such transplants.

If the United States decides, as a society, that all citizens have a right to most health care over the person's lifetime, then the only solution is a universal, single-payer model with all the positives and negatives involved with such a system. Costs to the individual would go down but waiting times would probably go up. In other nations with such systems, there still exists "boutique care" where the wealthy can pay for exceptional care. Think about the USA network show "Royal Pains" or a celebrity such as Teddy Kennedy or Steve Jobs. When Jobs required a liver transplant, he didn't have to wait. Or when Kennedy required special surgery for his brain tumor, he didn't have to wait. Nor did either man have to worry about costs or insurance payments. In point of fact, the U.S. Supreme Court would probably not allow a law which eliminates "boutique care." So inevitably, there will still be class differences even with universal care. The more important economic questions are: how is it paid for and is the average American willing to pay sufficient taxes to cover the costs of universal health care? Some of this has been answered by the passage of Medicare and Medicaid. Sentiment was high to cover seniors and the poor but no one really seemed to focus on the costs.

The United States ranks first in healthcare spending both in absolute dollars and as a percentage of GDP among nations of the world. The U.S. spends about 20 percent of its GDP on healthcare, about twice that of Germany, Canada, or Cuba among others. But what do citizens get for this money? U.S average life expectancy is under 80 years. Over 30 nations have life expectancies above 80 years. At least 30 nations have more doctors and hospital beds per capita. However, the U.S does rank above most nations in some health care statistics such as incidences of diabetes and obesity. The problem in the U.S. is that too much spending occurs on advanced health care technology and not enough is spent on a team approach and on preventive care. The nation is the envy of the world in technological prowess to cure someone when possible but you just have to get sick first. Numerous studies have shown preventive care is much cheaper than managing or curing the problem.

In a nation as big as the United States, with a population of 309 million, providing universal health care will be expensive and fraught with problems. However, not facing the problem will only exasperate it. The problem must be confronted now. Notwithstanding budgetary restraints, in order to have a coherent policy of national health care and insurance, a national health approach is necessary. Without such careful planning, America will be doomed to have both a failed national health program and a health sector with runaway costs. A continuation of the status quo will doom America to a second rate system.

## Present Situation in Health Care

The United States is in crisis with its huge fiscal deficit. Health care spending is a big part of the problem. Not only does America spend more of its GDP on health care, it is also increasing faster than almost any other expenditure. Rightly or wrongly, the U.S. Congress passed both Medicare and Medicaid to help two susceptible groups of the country, the aged and the poor. Now that these programs are part of the political landscape, the average citizen does not want to give them up. Polls show that about 80 percent of the American population wants these programs to continue. If they were not to continue, there would be two probable outcomes: for the poor, the hospital emergency rooms would once again be forced to accept patients who couldn't pay and this would just be factored into overall expenses and, for the aged, there would be some new government-sponsored program to cover them or else America would just have to write them off. In either case, it would be a terrible judgment against the richest country in the world.

But underlying all the present approaches is the fact that, without an overall approach to health care, the country will continue to spend more than it must and will spend it on a system that does not take a holistic approach to health care, an approach that could result in significantly lower costs. Many hospitals have found that where the team approach is taken, with full explanation and training to patients, the cure rates are better and the probability of recurring disease is much less.

Presently, personal selection and control seems to be the major objection to the new Obamacare plan. But what objection can there really be if the system is broken and just leaving it as is will not benefit anyone? The American public must decide if in fact the US wants better health care and if the US wants this health care to be universal. If the answer is "yes" to these questions, then the American public will have to accept that it may take more money to pay for such a system.

# CHAPTER IX

# BALANCING THE BUDGET

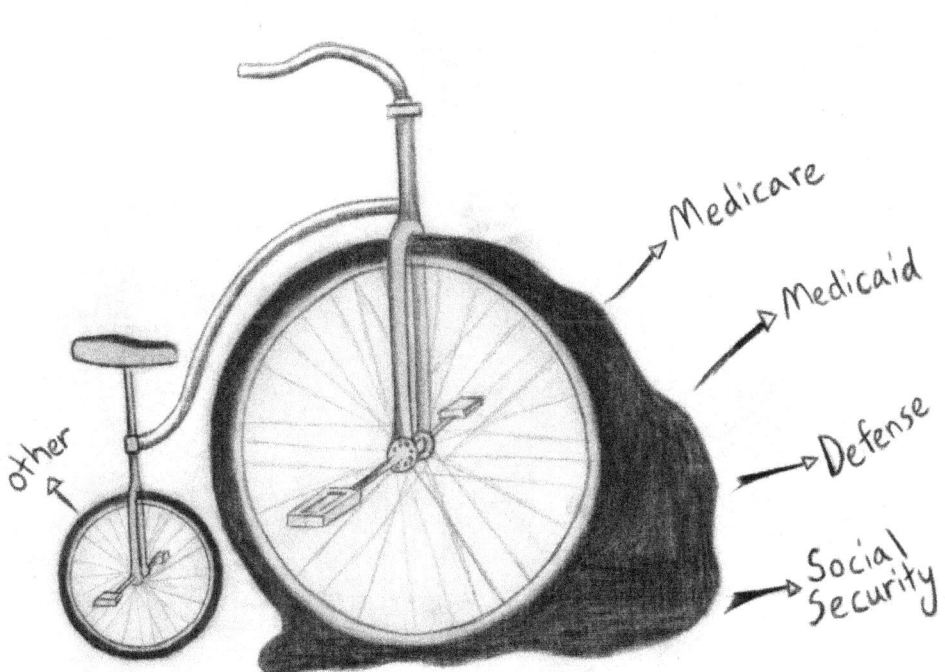

Medicare

Medicaid

Defense

Social Security

Other

*"As far as laws of mathematics refer to reality, they are not certain, and as far as they are certain, they do not refer to reality."*

ALBERT EINSTEIN

*"Entitlement spending – the politics of greed wrapped in the language of love."*

DICK ARMEY

*"At the time it is all confusion: in retrospect... it is all a blur."*

ARTHUR SCHLESINGER

*"No matter how thin you slice it, it's still baloney."*

AL SMITH

There was a huge surge in the federal deficit in the first two years of the Obama administration, largely as a result of the Great Recession. In 2010, as the economy was beginning to come out of its recession, much was discussed in heated terms about the deficit and cutting the federal budget. A new Tea Party was formed with a principle objective of cutting the budget. But when participants in the debate were questioned, few details were offered. As the old saying goes, "the devil is in the details."

Within the FY 2010 federal budget of $3.7 trillion only, $1.2 trillion or 33 percent was in discretionary, non-defense spending. Entitlements amounts were $1.5 trillion or 40 percent and defense was $700 billion or 19 percent of the total.

With the rhetoric at a fevered pitch as to the sacredness of not increasing taxes during an economic downturn, it became evermore evident that tax increases would be vigorously opposed. But when people spoke of Social Security and the probability of its going into the red and adding to the deficit, there were screams of alarm from the very strong retirement community, and rightly so. After all, for the seniors who worked all their lives and depend upon Social Security payments to maintain themselves, it is a matter of survival.

Although few want to admit it, there will almost certainly have to be some tax increases in the process of balancing the federal budget. And with certainty, any long-term fix will have to involve a high degree of austerity, living within one's means.

Cuts will have to be made across the board in order to balance the federal budget in the near future. With a budget of $3.7 trillion in 2010 and tax revenues of $2.4 trillion, the deficit was $1.3 trillion. In the following projections, (see projections at end of this chapter) there is a serious reduction in defense and a significant adjustment made to Social Security as well as tax increases. Proposals made by President Obama and others to freeze federal spending will reduce the deficit slightly but such reduction will only amount to less than 10 percent of the current deficit.

The Pandora's box of balancing the budget revolves around the desire to do such balancing with the detrimental tug of various, vested interests opposing programs cuts. In the end, we believe that world market forces will impose their will and the budget will be reduced and taxes will be raised.

While some argue that an improved economy will bring in more tax revenues and help to balance the budget, the numbers show this is unlikely. Even with an optimistic projection of growth, the results would be small. A balanced budget from this approach would take a long time to happen. If we assume the same tax structure, an economy increasing at 3.5 percent annual growth would add about $82 billion to tax receipts in the initial year, a small portion of the $1.3 trillion needed.

So, can you – our reader – best Congress and balance the budget? We're betting you can do it in under 30 minutes. This exercise splits the solution into choices of cuts in general spending, defense, entitlements, and tax increases. For each option, the budget at current levels is provided, rounded to the nearest $5 billion to make the arithmetic a little easier. By choosing a percentage of cut or percentage of taxes to increase for each option, see if you can reduce the deficit by $1 trillion. An option we propose shows the dollars cut or revenue raised in the 'amount saved' column. We reduced the deficit by $1.117 trillion. What choices would you make? Compare your solution with those of friends and family and see how similar – or not- they are.

Obviously, this exercise is highly simplified. The point is that to an individual, the math is simply not that hard; you cut $1 trillion in 30 minutes we're betting. But does your solution agree with that of others? That's the problem for congress – not the math, but agreement.

A Congressional committee is a group of people who individually can do nothing, but collectively decide nothing can be done.

## Debt Reduction and Revenue Increases

In the United States, the Democrats and Republicans have reached an impasse concerning bringing down the federal deficit. The Republicans led by the Tea Party activists have insisted on no new taxes. They want all reductions to come from shrinking the federal government. To this end, some 216 of new House of Representative members have signed a pledge of no new taxes. This forced House leader John Boehner to take an inflexible position. The Democrats have agreed to major budgetary reductions including entitlements but also have specified some tax increases. The tax increases they proposed are to eliminate tax loopholes while leaving the basic tax rates close to the rates prior to the Bush reductions. This would result in lower effective tax rates but an increase in overall tax revenues. The proposals were for spending cuts of $2 trillion over ten years with $400 billion dollars in new revenues from tax increases, creating a ratio of about 83/17. This was similar to a proposal in a Republican report of March 2011 which called for a split of 85/15 between budget cuts and new revenues. Throughout the time leading up to the lending limit deadline, the Republicans were intransigent and continually raised the ante. A mantra of the Tea Party activists has been CCB – cut, cap, and balance (cut the budget, cap the federal debt ceiling, and pass a constitutional amendment requiring a balanced budget). President Obama's position, which seems to have the support of a majority of Americans, was to have deficit reduction borne by all, not just the lower and middle classes. For this reason, Obama insisted upon tax revenue increases. However, it is critical to understand that Obama's proposals were to be implemented in 2013 to avoid handicapping the nascent economic recovery.

## Deleveraging

Much political posturing has surrounded talks of deficit reductions. In most cases, there is a major problem which the zealots do not seem ready to face. If there were an immediate balancing of the federal budget, it would result in reductions that would put the U.S. into a major economic tailspin. Immediate reduction of teachers, policemen, firemen, and other public service workers will have the dual effects of jeopardizing public sector safety and of raising unemployment when the U.S. is struggling to bring it down. The argument is that smaller government stimulates the creation of private sector jobs. This is only partially right. In the short term, the loss of public sector jobs cannot be regenerated by the private sector. Proposals to phase in any agreed budget reductions over a longer period would make more economic sense than sudden reductions. In a 2011 study by the McKinsey Global Institute, it was noted that, based on previous debt reduction episodes, rich countries that began deleveraging would need on average six to seven years to bring their debt levels down by about a quarter.

The McKinsey study shows that, after a financial crisis, countries have historically seen their economies contract in the first year or two of deleveraging. Thus, the method of deleveraging is itself important. Germany and Canada, for example, entered the crisis with relatively low levels of public and private debt. Their economies have consequently weathered deleveraging better than other developed countries. On the other hand, Italy, France, and Japan entered the recession with low household debt but high levels of government borrowing. Both France and Italy have therefore been able to stimulate growth with less deleveraging. Japan began what appeared to be well-reasoned deleveraging but the earthquake and tsunami disrupted its recovery. Spain, Britain, and the United States have the worst of both worlds. They have dangerously stretched household balance sheets and, because of the decrease in private sector activity and large stimulus attempts, their public books are also in disarray. Notwithstanding this, American households have reduced their debt to 112 percent of annual disposable income, down from 127 percent. This is a two-edged sword, resulting in lower consumer spending at this critical recovery stage in the United States. Tellingly, in both Spain and Britain, the sober deficit reduction plans adopted by these countries have severely impacted households' expectations of real disposable income. If plans are put into effect such as those recommended by the International Monetary Fund (IMF) for the United States, with the structural deficit being reduced to 7.5 percent of GDP by 2016, this would have the effect of trimming 0.5 to 0.75 percentage points off average growth over the period.

There are four lessons to be learned from the deleveraging efforts up to now. First, that in many cases, when large debt reduction is required, some orderly write-downs are required. The large mortgage foreclosures in the United States are an example and may have saved many years of less extreme but more corroding write-downs. Second, nominal growth is essential to bring down large debt loads. This may entail higher inflation than normal. Thus, public sector austerity may need to be calibrated to the scale of private deleveraging. America should look for a medium-term deficit reduction plan rather than a short-term plan that would set the private sector retrenchment back at a critical moment. Third, the best way to soften the pain of deleveraging is with an export led recovery. To do this may require a rebalancing of currencies with the emerging Asian countries strengthening their currencies and the developed world weakening theirs. This will also entail China strengthening its consumer society and reallocating resources toward tradable goods and services with such economies as the United States and the rich countries of Europe. But fourth, the depressing lesson of deleveraging is the reality that it will be painful. Almost universally, economists are saying that the rich economies will have some years of retrenching, some difficult years both politically and economically.

## *Present Situation*

So the issue for politicians is "pick your poison" for providing the fundamental services that the federal government should give. If the amount totals more than current tax revenues, then tax revenue increases are required to balance the budget. Remember that, as pointed out in the chapter on taxation, revenue increases do not necessarily require rate increases. However, any services currently provided by the federal government, beyond the ones that the nation decides are fundamental, are fair game for cutting or eliminating. States that "take up the slack" will have to decide how to pay for expanded services. There will never be total agreement among politicians and citizens as to how to balance the budget. Indeed, we as a nation will know the best compromise when we see it and no one will be happy with it! The choice is one of how much unhappiness is acceptable.

The Tea Party movement has brought a focus on the balancing of the U.S. budget. Both Republican and Democrats seem to agree that there is an emergency that must be resolved. However, there is a dichotomy in the philosophy of how to solve the problem. One side seems to say, "We must take drastic steps right now." Outside of the U.S. lies another reality. If the

U.S. doesn't put its fiscal house in order voluntarily, then the world markets may force them to do so in a fashion that will be far more painful and less amenable to America.

As can be seen from analyzing the detail, it will require a combination of both cost and program cutting and tax increases to bring the federal budget back to some semblance of balance. For this to occur, America will need to push its politicians into taking some drastic steps. With such steps, there will be certain pain. However, without taking these steps, the outlook is far more dismal and will be far more painful.

We invite you to study the following proposal to see how you might balance the budget.

## POTENTIAL CUTS/INCREASES TO BALANCE BUDGET AS OF FY 2011

| Overall CUT S | Billions | | | |
|---|---|---|---|---|
| GENERAL SPENDING CUTS | 140 | See | Detail | A |
| DEFENSE CUTS | 287 | See | Detail | B |
| ENTITLEMENT CUTS | 420 | See | Detail | C |
| TAX INCREASES | 270 | See | Detail | D |
| GRAND TOTAL | 1,117 | | | |

# GENERAL SPENDING CUTS

## DETAIL A

| Item | Budget in Billions | Percentage Cut | Amount Saved in Billions |
|---|---|---|---|
| • Federally paid Civilian Workers | 300 | 15 | 45 |
| • Federal Aid to | 200 | 10 | 20 |
| • States | | | |
| • Federal Workforce | 150 | 10 | 15 |
| • Foreign Aid | 30 | 80 | 24 |
| • Farm Subsidies | 15 | 100 | 15 |
| • Earmarks | 15 | 100 | 15 |
| • Federal Contractors | 15 | 20 | 3 |
| • Other (Parks,Education) | 30 | 10 | 3 |
| TOTAL | 755 | | 140 |

## Detail B

## DEFENSE

| Item | Budget in Billions | Percentage Cut | Amount Saved in Billions |
|---|---|---|---|
| • Eliminate all Active-duty Military Personnel | 325 | 10 | 32 |
| • End Wars in Iraq + Afghanistan | 200 | 100 | 200 |
| • Reduce non-combat Compensation | 50 | 10 | 5 |
| • Reduce Nuclear Arsenal | 40 | 50 | 20 |
| • Reduce Navy and Air Force Fleets | 25 | 40 | 10 |
| • Cancel Weapons Programs not contracted | 20 | 100 | 20 |
| TOTAL | 655 | | 287 |

## Detail C

# ENTITLEMENT CUTS

| Item | Budget (Billions) | % cut | Amount Saved in Billions |
|------|------|------|------|
| • Cap Medicare Growth at GDP (rationing) | 600 | 20 | 120 |
| • Increase Medicare eligibility to age 70 | 105 | 0 | 0 |
| • Malpractice Reform | 15 | 100 | 15 |
| • Raise Social Security eligibility to age 70 | 240 | 100 | 240 |
| • Reduce Social Security COLA to inflation | 80 | 50 | 40 |
| • Reduce growth of starting Social Security benefits | 55 | 0 | 0 |
| • Increase disability eligibility | 15 | 0 | 0 |
| TOTAL | 1,115 | | 420 |

# Detail D

## TAX INCREASES

| ITEM | Budget in Billions | Fraction increase implemented | Amt Saved bns |
|---|---|---|---|
| • Estate tax after $ 1,000,000 | 105 | 0 | 0 |
| • Investment income as ordinary income | 55 | 0 | 0 |
| • Let Bush tax cuts on everyone expire ($100 Bn increase for just over $250,000 is 40% of total) | 250 | 40 | 100 |
| • Apply FICA tax to all income | 100 | 100 | 100 |
| • Cut tax deductions for mortgage interest state taxes, etc | 350 | 20 | 70 |
| • National 10% Sales tax | 600 | 0 | 0 |
| TOTAL | 1, 460 | | 270 |

# CHAPTER X

# HOUSING

*"How many things I can do without."*

SOPHOCLES

*"Practical efficiency is common, and lofty idealism is not uncommon; it is the combination that is necessary, and that combination is rare."*

FRANKLIN D. ROOSEVELT

*"Merely to adopt the more powerful assumption is no more than to assume the more powerful conclusion."*

ROBERT SOLOW

U ntil recently, the American public believed home ownership was a God-given right, something all Americans deserved - a birthright. Through the 1950's, the average American family consisted of one income earner, usually the father with the mother staying at home and being the homemaker or center of the family. A house was a central part of this scene. Television programs such as "Leave it to Beaver," "Father Knows Best," and "The Adventures of Ozzie and Harriett," all spoke to this ideal family structure. Veterans coming home from World War II or Korea would buy a dream, houses built by Levitt, which although little more than crackerjack boxes, were their own. This model was idealistically perfect because of where America was at the time, a society in which the father worked at one job for his whole life – paying the bills, so when he and his wife retired, they would have a paid off mortgage. The home was both a consumption item and the kingdom where the family resided.

But, this all changed as the American family structure changed toward the end of the 20th century. Women no longer stayed at home. They became part of the workforce, persons with their own earnings and lives apart from being a wife and mother. In fact, many households became single-parent units, evolving to the present situation where 50 percent of American children live in single-parent households. Additionally, it no longer was the norm for a person to hold one job with one company his or her whole life. Some statistics show the average American would hold seven different jobs in his or her lifetime.

In this evolution of American society, the purpose of home ownership changed radically. Today, while a house is still a consumption item because it represents shelter, it also has become an investment, but not an investment as it had been in the first part of the 20th century. Now, it is often a speculation in which it doesn't matter if one lives in the house as it's assumed that, based on a half century of economic history, the value of the house would automatically increase each and every year. As American society became increasingly consumer-oriented, it also became a society in which savings was less and less part of the norm. By the 1990's, America had a savings rate (less whatever was being accumulated in their houses) that was negative. In simple terms, Americans were not saving but were borrowing to maintain their consumer lifestyles. This came to its epitome during the George W. Bush presidency, reaching its height and partially causing the spectacular economic crash of 2008.

This Great Recession that began in December 2007 brought economic uncertainty as to the investment value of home purchases. Starting in the 1990's, easy money - combined with some sleight of hand by Wall Street - made mortgage money available with few of the conventional banking safeguards. Financial qualification with employment verification was re-laxed. In the past, a general rule of thumb was that a person would have to be making enough money so that the mortgage payment was no more than 20 to 25 percent of income. Furthermore, a substantial down pay-ment of at least 20 percent of the cost of the home was required. But Wall Street and the new quants (quantitative analysts) invented financial instru-ments by packaging mortgages together and spinning them off to special off-balance sheet entities that were supposed to eliminate the risk. Credit default swaps (CDS) were sold, guaranteeing someone would pick up the losses if there was default. Subprime loans (loans made without enough down payment or without the party having enough demonstrable income) were packaged together and spun off in new vehicles in which good and bad loans would offset one another. The famous bell curve would rule, in which the tails would be offset by the great center of the curve. Then in-surance sold by such firms as AIG, and even major banks such as Morgan Chase and Citibank, would cover dubious subprime mortgages. Lenders all over the world began to buy the new mortgage instruments being offered by American banks. This, combined with the cheap money of the U.S. Federal Reserve System, kept funds flowing into the burgeoning American mortgage market. Other countries and financial markets began duplicating this new, "magic" formula. Behind it all, the driving force was profit as the instruments issued paid fat fees. Since banks were spinning the packaged mortgages off to these new special purpose vehicles, the liabilities did not appear on their balance sheets so their loan-to-capital ratios were never in question.

Although the CDS market was difficult to measure in full, since most deals between the guaranteeing agency or bank and the purchasing agency or bank were private transactions not recorded on any recognized financial exchange or market, one estimate is that the nominal value of these CDS's grew to over $13 trillion dollars by the time of the Great Recession. The problem was there was not enough money behind it all to guarantee liquidity in the case of a run.

When the inevitable collapse began, it was found that many of those U.S. houses that increased annually in value by 10 percent or more were no longer worth the money they were financed for. The famous "under water" home materialized in which the mortgage balance was greater than the house was worth. The natural result was that many owners began to walk away from their home rather than to keep paying mortgages on homes not worth the balance owed. One effect of the bursting of the housing bubble was a significant decrease in the average price of homes in America with values plunging 30, 40, or even 50 percent depending on location.

This phenomenon got its push in both the Clinton and Bush presidencies. Home ownership was "all-American" and builders were constructing houses in record numbers with lenders providing mortgages without regards to affordability in all too many cases. Families were buying houses on a speculative basis without thinking of the consequences of possible market changes. As prices soared, many households used equity loans or lines of credit to draw on the new wealth being created by rising home prices. Lower interest rates and introductory deals as well as cash-out refinancing made these loans affordable as long as house prices continued to rise and interest rates were fixed. When variable rate loans adjusted upward, payments became unaffordable for many. A rise in foreclosures began to push prices down. The negative consequences spread to the "prime" market from the "sub-prime" market. This was the beginning of the bursting of the bubble. The housing crisis unfolded and became a full-fledged financial crisis.

The American dream of home ownership for all began to fall apart. Renting became part of the landscape once again. Since, in the new America, a person will be changing his or her job about seven times in his or her lifetime, it seems to make sense to rent rather than purchase with the risk of house prices falling. Renting gives this flexibility, whereas house ownership, while it brings profits in rising markets, also ties a person down if markets are falling or stagnant. Home ownership restricts a person if he or she is offered a job across the country. Compounding the situation is the specter of unemployment and the problem of getting stuck with a house with high fixed monthly mortgage payments. So, for the first time in fifty years, it is making economic sense to rent rather than to buy for a large number of households.

From a government policy perspective, does encouraging home ownership through various subsidies make sense? There is not enough money in the commercial banking system to carry all the mortgages of American home ownership. This is where Fannie Mae and Freddie Mac come in. They repurchase home mortgages and, without them, the private banking system could not handle the American demand for home mortgage financing. Yet, in the 2008 crisis, it turned out that these quasi-governmental agencies held a great deal of bad paper and incurred significant losses when writing down these bad loans. The federal government subsidizes housing in other ways. It makes interest payments on home loans, as well as property taxes, income tax deductible. Federal Reserve policy in repurchasing Treasury issues has pushed long-term interest rates to the lowest level in decades. Such low rates stimulated house investment and suppressed savings since Americans saw no incentive in keeping savings in low-yielding bank instruments when they could be in high-earning real estate. All of these factors effect the allocation of resources and cause money to flow to home ownership. The assumption was that home ownership was socially positive. There is no doubt that the economic effects from this housing boom in the 1990's were great. Demand for everything from raw materials such as lumber, glass, brick, siding, and so on to furniture, appliances, and other consumer durables was stimulated by the housing boom. But, on the other side of the equation, Americans were not saving at all and funding for other productive investments such as factories, technologies, and research was less available, especially when competing with government demand for available funds.

In the modern American economy, the question becomes what should the role of the government be in stimulating home ownership. It could be that in the new America, home ownership will no longer have the importance it had to family life in the past. America may more appropriately begin to realize that resources such as home ownership must be rethought with new emphasis on other means of savings.

# Continuing Role of Fannie Mae and Freddie Mac

Central to the federal government's housing focus has been the use of two government sponsored enterprises (GSEs), Fannie Mae and Freddie Mac. Under the present system, these two institutions buy mortgages from banks and repackage them for sale to investors. Although they are in one sense separate from the federal government as private individuals own their stock, bondholders believed there was an implied guarantee where the government would rescue them should they run into trouble. So, in order to finance their purchases of mortgages, they issued bonds which, because of the implicit guarantee, enjoyed extremely favorable interest rates, making their mortgage purchase arrangement feasible. With the financial meltdown and subprime crisis of 2008-10, the government was forced to take over both institutions in 2008. About half of the $10.6 trillion home mortgages of the United States were involved.

Since the government takeover in 2008, there has been about $134 billion in losses to the two institutions. Unfortunately, primarily due to the quantity of mortgages (especially subprime mortgages), taxpayers have been called upon to finance another $500 billion to pay for further losses the government suffered through Fannie and Freddie.

The major criticism has been that the government never received adequate compensation for the risk it assumed. This developed because, in 1992, the government required GSEs to extend their subsidy to low income borrowers who couldn't meet the standards for subprime loans. On top of this, in 2008, the Congress allowed both institutions to buy mortgages for million-dollar homes. When the housing market imploded in 2008-10, the GSEs got slammed from both the subprime loans and from the high end mortgages.

The Obama Administration is now proposing to lower the support, reducing maximum loans from $729,750 to $625,500, to increase minimum down payments to 10 percent for loans eligible for purchase by Fannie and Freddie, and to increase the premiums charged on loans backed by the Federal Housing Administration.

Presently, with the political rhetoric for reducing the deficit and moving the government out of as many activities as possible, there are three proposals on the table: 1) put the vast majority of the mortgage loans in the private sector where lenders would originate the mortgages and securitize them without any government backing this approach would eliminate the role played by Fannie and Freddie, 2) create a mostly private market with a limited government backstop that would only become active in buying or guaranteeing loans in periods when private lenders retreated because of financial shocks, or 3) create new privately-owned companies to buy mortgages from the banks and resell them as securities. These securities would be explicitly guaranteed by the government as long as they met certain criteria and the government would charge fees similar to what is charged by the FDIC to insure bank deposits.

There is general agreement that the froth must be removed from the present system and that most people in the U.S., who seek home ownership (probably over 85 percent) have FICO credit scores of more than 720 – the dividing line between a prime and subprime borrower. Currently, the pendulum has swung too far the other way, with home loans too hard and too costly in down payments and closing costs even for worthy home buyers.

What this comes down to is that the misfocused policy of universal home ownership, that opened mortgages to subprime or otherwise risky loans, would be revised. While this may prevent the goal of universal home ownership, it would restabilize the system so that home ownership and mortgage granting was on a more realistic and viable basis.

Once again, we stress that no one is helped by programs doomed to failure because of shaky economic thinking. U.S. housing in 2008 exemplified social thinking based on a shaky economic foundation. The questions always should be what do we want, what is the cost, and how will it be paid for.

# CHAPTER XI

# EDUCATION

Chapter XI
EDUCATION
(Left Behind)

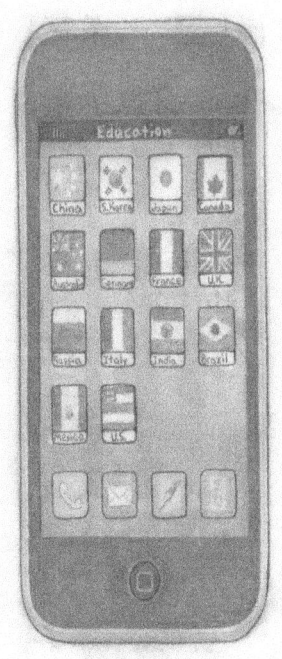

*"The unexamined life is not worth living."*

SOCRATES

*"There is only one good, knowledge; and one evil, ignorance."*

SOCRATES

*"All men naturally desire knowledge."*

ARISTOTLE

*"Science can only state what is, not what should be."*

ALBERT EINSTEIN

*"Education is hanging on until you have caught on."*

ROBERT FROST

The extent and depth of the United States crisis of 2007-10 can best be exemplified by the education crisis. The structural problems in American education are demonstrated by such symptoms as: the Detroit public school system where one-third of its schools were forced to close in 2009 and almost 50 percent of its high school students were not graduating, or of national teachers starting salaries at around $37,000, or of a federal budget for education only amounting to 9 percent of the total cost of education, or of education expenditures only accounting for about 2 percent of GDP. These are some of the very real structural problems in American education.

Public education - primary and secondary schooling - is over 91 percent funded on a local level, primarily by property taxes on the community. Quite naturally, the richer districts will have better schooling than the poorer districts. Furthermore, the nation is divided into more than 95,000 school districts with virtually no cohesive national policy.

The educational problems are at the very heart of the structural employment problems the nation is facing. In order to remain the world's economic leader, or even to remain competitive in a world with emerging economic giants such as China and India, the nation must change its educational systems dramatically. Optimal success will be realized when children begin to complain about having to go to school on weekends rather than complaining about hours spent on weekdays! As it stands, students in other developing countries with much scarcer resources, are attending schools in shifts and, in some countries, science graduates are outnumbering U.S. science graduates as a percentage of total graduates by 10 to 1. In Latin America, in at least two countries, subsidies are being offered to the very poorest to send their children to school. In India, its technological schools are so good that a major U.S. company sent some of its executives there to study. America, which has always prided itself on its quality universities, is now facing the problem of students in the lower school systems not being adequately prepared to begin college.

Education must have two overriding goals: to create a "well rounded" citizen and to prepare that person for economic success in life. Without a first rate educational system, a nation's readiness to have an economy that takes advantage of rapidly morphing technology is limited. A first rate education system begins in kindergarten. Children must enjoy school and work at the tasks of learning "reading, writing, and arithmetic" in which they are being prepared for the next steps of education, but also in ways so they can see such subjects as relevant to them. A child, at about the fifth or sixth grade level, begins to ask the teacher, "How am I going to use this in real life?" The teacher should have a reasonable, pertinent, and ready response. In Denmark, this concept is taken to the extreme with children as early as 5 and 6 years old being analyzed and groomed as to what professions they should be prepared for, with a long-term plan made for them.

Obviously, all schools - public, private or charter - should be safe for both children and teachers. They must be free from drugs, from gang and other violence, and in well-maintained and physically attractive settings. They must present an environment conducive to learning in which students willingly come and participate. Questionable "zero tolerance" policies, such as expelling children for bringing Tylenol to school, should be eliminated in favor of common sense approaches that don't reek of compulsion but rather of children/parent/teacher cooperation in reasonable ways to guarantee a stimulating learning environment.

Taking a page from U.S. history, education spending and support must continue to come from the local level. There can be no substitute for parent-teacher meetings or for local school boards running the schools. A Washington-style, one-size-fits all approach is doomed to failure. But, there must also be increasing use of national testing criteria and evaluation methodology. Maybe the most important thing that will revitalize American education is a new focus on pay and meritorious rewards to superior teachers. A grand design must be found where outstanding teachers are recognized and rewarded while inferior teachers are dismissed and replaced. In order to do this, pay must be raised, including starting pay, to attract the very best minds to teaching. Ways must be found of keeping teachers in the classroom but not as surrogate parents, security guards, paper pushers, or authors of largely useless, bureaucratic reports. Innovation in these areas will do the most to improve the system and promote teaching by motivated and superior teachers, lifting the educational level more rapidly than any other single thing.

Students should also use technology to improve knowledge access. Computer-based learning must be utilized to maximum advantage with such new technological gadgets as e-book readers and tablets. Students must become excited and techniques such as texting, Facebook, or Shout-It-Out should be incorporated into the education curriculum.

A revamped and rejuvenated education system is crucial if the nation is to advance in a world where technology and knowledge-based jobs provide the best salaries. The country must have a well-educated workforce to compete with China, India, and other rapidly developing nations whose focus is on preparing its young for professions with a laser sharp focus. In the U.S., students and adults fall far behind in mathematics and the sciences, the very areas needed for the change fundamental to success in this technical world. A flower requires a STEM (Science, Technology, Engineering, and Mathematics) to blossom!

Even with a focus on the sciences and mathematics, there must be a parallel focus on vocational and niche preparation. In Germany, apprenticeship programs are parallel with university training. Young people serve anywhere from 6 to 10 years learning to be a master carpenter or a master plumber, to be a tool and die maker, or to be a well-trained municipal worker or city planner. Pay and status follow in the work life of its young people who are prepared by such intensive apprenticeship efforts.

In addition to the focus on mathematics and science, there must be a renewed effort at language education. With a society in which Spanish is increasingly becoming a second U.S. language, students should be given enough language training at a young age when the mind is open to such learning. Then, by the time a student has completed his primary education, he or she will be on a bilingual path. Our neighbors in Latin America educate their students in English so that most of their secondary school graduates have some conversational abilities. Other languages like Mandarin Chinese, Russian, or Portuguese (spoken in Brazil) should be offered.

In a world of Facebook, Twitter, Shout It Out, and 3D movies, these technologies must be used to excite and turn on young minds. This is part of the relevancy we speak of in this chapter. Science must become fun as opposed to being a "nerd thing." History, art, civics, economics, and literature must become vibrant and alive. Rote learning by repetition must be replaced by dynamic, differentiated, and robust lesson plans with computerized learning methods to augment interest and make subject matter relevant to students. Comprehension of content, learned through holistic reading methods, should be central. Should high school physics cover the "simple machines" or would an elementary discussion of particle physics and the nature of the universe be more likely to inspire a budding physicist? Unless more students become excited about learning, they won't become successful adults in a global economy where they are directly pitted against Chinese and Indian youth who have received more intensive training. This will not happen until our schools become exciting places of learning, places where much is demanded of the student and the student is challenged, where "boring" and a "waste of time" disappear from the student lexicon.

But we cannot place it all on the shoulders of the teachers and students. Leading American educators are preaching parental involvement. Geoffrey Canada, of Harlem's Save the Children program, stresses full parental participation. Both he and the school teachers visit the parents. If a student is doing badly or is truant, they go to the parent and get them involved in making sure the student improves. Canada is striving for a 100 percent graduation rate for his students. And, he expects 75 percent of the students to go on to college. What makes this so amazing is that this is occurring with economically-deprived children. Lotteries are held for spots in his school. Parents strive to get their children in his school as a means of giving them a better life. The nation must strive to eliminate high school or vocational school dropouts, for this represents failure. America will continue to flourish only if its citizens are world-prepared.

College is another matter. There are many functions in society that don't require a college education. For some people, jobs in a K-Mart, jobs as a medical technician, or any number of manual jobs will allow them to earn a maintenance level wage. But this is the students' choice and should be so after attaining a high school education.

The high school graduate will have several options. First, she may take a job with a lower wage where she can move into better paying, possibly supervisory jobs. Second, she may proceed to college and pursue a major subject or profession in something, which can be profitable, and for which she feels suited. Such a student may continue to graduate school to gain a post graduate degree in law, medicine, the sciences, liberal arts, or an advanced business degree. Such choices should be made based on actual market conditions of demand and wages but also on aptitude and personality characteristics. Third, the student who graduates high school may proceed to a vocational school to learn a skilled trade. The nation will always need hands on persons doing such things as carpentry, plumbing, electrical work, etc.

In the America of the mid 20th century, all high schools had practical shop courses to give students a feel for trade work. In Denmark, a small but sophisticated nation off the German coast, society begins to analyze children at young ages and to direct them to different levels of work careers. The state will subsidize a child with great potential who comes from a lower socio-economic family.

Educational institutions should make clear to students what job opportunities are available and what wages they pay. This information will allow students facing a choice of a major in computer sciences or philosophy to make a career choice based on real life factors. This intensive guidance will also allow students to make the critical decisions of whether they wish to proceed to graduate school, law school, or medical school. Students should make such life-forming decisions with as much information as possible. Academics can argue that it is unfair that the philosophy student averages a lower wage than a computer science major but the argument is irrelevant to the student's choice. The high school graduate, who proceeds to a technical school or continues such training begun in high school, should be shown what job opportunities lay before him or her in the vocational profession of their choice and what wages they can expect.

# Education Reform

Educational reform does not require significantly more funding but it does require that funding be redirected so that real reform is made. According to the Organization of Economic Cooperation and Development (OECD), per pupil spending rose by 123 percent in the U.S. from 1971 through 2006 and helped to reduce the student-to-teacher ratio from 22:1 to 16:1, a 27 percent decrease. But academic performance has simply not improved. The United States ranks in the bottom 20 percent of developed countries in math and science. More than a quarter of eighth graders score at a "below basic" level in reading and math while fewer than 10 percent score "advanced" in either subject. So high schools and colleges must spend time teaching remedial reading and math to students. The change needed is one of attitude. Parental, business, and governmental involvement is crucial. Since all parties agree on the importance of education and that change is required, surely agreement on how to achieve such change can be reached. Innovative, local strategies can and must be possible. Such a focus is necessary to offer our youth an opportunity in the global economy and to allow the United States to continue to compete as a leading economic power.

## Specific Change

Some specific changes could be made that would have immediate results. A national fund to bring budgets of poorer districts in line with wealthier districts could be implemented. This could be funded on a national basis but managed on a state and local basis. A national policy of meritorious pay for outstanding teachers should be devised and implemented to reward superior teaching. This would be run in concurrence with a policy dismissing poor teachers. Teachers' unions and school administrators would have to work together in such an effort. A general increase in teaching salaries, both in starting pay and in annual increases for performance, should be promoted. Both federal and state funding should be used to do this as this goes much beyond local schools and is, in fact, a national issue of highest priority. A national job corps, much like the Peace Corps, could be started with 2 to 4 year volunteer periods and automatic payoff or cancellation of any student loans of the volunteers. The young people could be sent to poorer communities and could be used in pilot programs. A national vocational and technological school fund should be established with funding drawn from corporate and private sector donors. Some federal seed money could also be used. The fund would be used for supplying computers, advanced software, and other educational training machines and computer systems. A national network of technological schools and vocational programs added to existing high schools should be created. Such a network would promote apprenticeship programs and would be run on a private basis but would be supported by both private and corporate funding as well as some federal funding. Lastly, a national campaign promoting education should be started much like the anti-drug programs of past years and should be funded and developed with intensive advertising campaigns.

## Present Situation

In the panic to balance budgets, the states are beginning to cut public services. Unfortunately, they are cutting education. Some cutting is appropriate, such as what's being done with reference to pension funding. However, the overall focus should be on improving education, not on cost cutting. Better education will inevitably involve more funding rather than less funding. If the local and state governments cannot afford funding for education, then the federal government will have to assist both at the local and state levels.

Major changes must be made, such as those suggested in this chapter. It has been accepted that about 1,800 high schools nationwide are substandard with the majority of their students dropping out. President Obama has visited several of these schools and the federal government has focused on helping them restructure themselves. The three recommendations being made for reforming them are: 1) closing them down and transferring the students to other successful schools, 2) changing the principals while reviewing and improving teachers, and 3) changing the schools to charter schools. In all cases, the substandard schools cannot continue as they currently exist. America's children are suffering because they are not receiving an adequate education.

But, it must be emphasized that cost cutting is not the issue and will in fact make a bad situation worse. Probably one of the worst public school systems in the United States is in Detroit, a city devastated by the economic turndown. A new man was put in as a special troubleshooter to bring education cost down. He began by closing schools, eliminating bad teachers, and initiating a series of streamlining measures. The result was an improvement in the education system but no reduction in costs. This exemplifies that cost saving is not the issue, rather the quality of education is. Focusing on eliminating inefficiencies is important to reform but the more important action is to get excellent teachers teaching and to get parents and communities involved. In this, the Harlem Children's Project is a sterling example. Geoffrey Canada has created a system for the very poorest children to get a quality education and his system aims for a 100 percent high school graduation rate.

Education is probably the area of greatest crisis in America and both budgetary and structurally more, rather than less, emphasis and resources should be given to bringing America's public education system back to first class. The future of the country lies with educating our children in a competitive world class system.

# CHAPTER XII

# INCARCERATION

(The New Gulag - 2,500,000 American Prisoners)

*"It is not in the end the prisoners who are destroyed, even though they may lose their lives. It is the jailers, and it is the oppressors who are doomed... tyrants have been trying to crush the Russian dedication to human ideals for so many years that it is hard to know when the efforts first began. They may not have succeeded. Solzhenitsyn is testimony to their failure."*

HARRISON SALISBURY

*"You only have power over people so long as you do not take everything from them. But when you have robbed man of everything, he is free."*

ALEXANDER SOLZHENITSYN

*"The rights of all men are diminished when the rights of one man are threatened."*

JOHN F KENNEDY

*"And were an epitaph to be my story, I'd have a short one as my own. I would have written on my stone, I had a lover's quarrel with the world."*

ROBERT FROST

Amerca is different from the rest of the world. It has much good to be admired but also has bad to be avoided. One of the bad things is the propensity to lock up its people. America now has more prisoners than any developed country in history, both in total and as a proportion of population. About one out of every 100 of its adult citizens is involved with the justice system. A total of over 2,300,000 people are incarcerated in American prisons (federal, state, county, armed forces, local jails). Its incarcerated population now exceeds the total population of 15 of its states. Compared with other rich countries, America far exceeds them. The rate of incarceration in Britain is one fifth that of America's, in Germany it's one ninth of America's, and in Japan one twelfth of America's.

About four decades ago crime and incarceration became an emotive issue in America and voters took to backing politicians who promised to stamp out crime. This ratcheted up into lawmakers campaigning on being tough on crime and getting popular support from their citizenry. These lawmakers then formulated tougher laws. The politicians who didn't sound tough on crime lost elections. It became a bellwether issue. Logic and a clear-cut policy to protect society while administering a level, just and well-applied judicial philosophy became a system in which the "Dirty Harry" approach dominated. A tough-on-criminals-at-any-cost philosophy controlled national politics. The philosophy of innocent until proven guilty disappeared and the new philosophy was guilty until proven innocent. Even when a defendant is found not guilty, the public often reacts negatively without having been in the courtroom to hear the evidence, as demonstrated in the recent Casey Anthony case. Softness in the courts is frowned upon. It is much easier to get voters behind a candidate who says, "I will not pander to the criminals; I will give them what they deserve; I will lock them up and throw away the key." When the young rebelled, when the minorities claimed rights, when people who were not understood by the average citizen broke a rule, the motto was we will try them to the maximum degree of the law and put them in jail.

In other parts of the world, similar things were happening but not to the same degree as in America. Over the same time frame, in Britain the rate of incarceration doubled and in Japan it increased by half. However, the trend in America, the richest country, was far in excess of any other nation. The questions became whether America has a greater propensity to criminality and whether this tough on crime policy is an effective determinant to criminality. Neither seems to be the case. It is doubtful whether any of the developed or rich societies has more criminally-oriented citizens than another. Statistics don't support the detrimental factor.

America has evolved into a country that locks up its young offenders, who it considers the most prone to commit further crimes for increasingly longer periods of time. This has been codified with what are called "mandatory minimum sentences" – sentences which must be imposed regardless of whether a judge and the facts argue for a lesser sentence. Mercy and humanitarian considerations have been removed. Those to the political right have characterized anyone espousing such liberality as "soft" or as people who simply don't understand the realities of life.

Added to this is what has become a hodgepodge of laws. America imprisons people for technical violations of immigration laws, for environmental violations, for breaking arcane business laws, for small quantities of what it has defined as illicit drugs. So many federal rules have been passed in America that it is almost impossible to count them all. Many are incomprehensible. Few are ever repealed. As it presently stands, the United States now has more criminal laws than any other nation in the world. There are laws for depriving the public of "the intangible right of honest services." There are laws in which a criminal defendant can be charged and augmented for the same crime by dividing it into various incidents of wire fraud, illicit drug sales, etc. Prosecutors love these laws, for they can get easy prosecutions and build a record. Law enforcement and U.S. prosecutors have built a system where the informant now is the basic tool for developing and prosecuting a case. Thus, with the testimony of a man or woman who was involved in a crime, cases are developed leading to indictments for the crime of conspiracy and the witness is given a reward of a lesser sentence or, in many cases, no prosecution for the same crime. This has pushed the success rate of prosecutions to 97 percent in federal cases. With mandatory minimum laws and the easily proven conspiracy charge, many defendants plead guilty rather than risk a trial. In fact, if one goes to trial to defend his or her innocence and loses, he or she will receive a much stiffer sentence. In other words, a defendant will be castigated for trying to defend himself or herself.

In 1989, federal parole was eliminated. Sentences were to be served for 85 percent of the total. It didn't matter what the defendant did, what his background was, or how much he demonstrated rehabilitation while incarcerated, he or she had to serve 85 percent of his or her entire sentence. This was supposed to bring more equality in sentencing. But, what occurred was sentences became greater than before, and even when the same, they were, in effect, much longer since there was no early release for good behavior. So what happened in the past 20 years since the new law came into effect is the federal prison population aged dramatically. Even with a greater number of young prisoners, there is a skewing of the average age of prisoners with a tremendously swelling number of "gray beards." The cost of maintenance of these older prisoners also swelled to where it now consumes over 25 percent of prison budgets. Some 200,000 of the 2,300,000 prisoners are over 50 years of age and it is not uncommon to see men in their 70's and even 80's going to federal prison.

## Major Flaws

By most penologists' analyses, the U.S. system of criminal justice has three major flaws: (1) it puts too many people away for too long, (2) it criminalizes acts that need not be criminalized, and (3) it is unpredictable.

In 1970, an average of one in 400 Americans was in prison. Now, that number is one in 100. As it appeared that violent crime was going up, the number of laws and prison time increased geometrically. When drug addiction seemed to be rising, it became an easy target and the harshest laws possible were passed. Minorities especially felt the brunt of this new focus. There are now more young Black men in America in prison than in college. And a glance at any federal prison shows over two-thirds of its population is Black or Hispanic. Again the question must be asked, is it because of predisposition to crime or are minorities a target of the system?

New laws have removed much of judges' discretion while sentences are harsher and must be served in their entirety. Because no politician wants to be viewed as soft on crime, mandatory minimum laws are seldom lowered. On the contrary, they tend to get harsher.

Some criminals belong behind bars for long periods. When a habitual rapist is locked up, the streets are safer. But the same cannot be said for a petty drug dealer, or a petty thief, whose incarceration fills a space for someone who terrorizes society and should be locked up. Since the new laws came into effect in 1989, the number of drug offenders locked up in federal and state prisons has increased 13-fold.

When the federal government removed parole, it pressured the states to do the same by withholding federal aid to those states that didn't rescind their parole policy. However, along with rescinding parole, the new sentencing in America extended probation to ever longer periods. Thus, a man or woman who served his or her sentence is under "correctional supervision" for continued periods after release - another 10, 15, or even 20 years. When factoring in these people, America now has one in every 31 adults under some kind of penal custody. This has resulted in two things: extreme overcrowding in many states and federal prisons and an explosion of the overall costs of incarceration.

## Cost Explosion

With 2,300,000 people incarcerated in America, the total cost of such incarceration now exceeds $125 billion annually. Out of this total, however, only about $8 billion is for federal prisoners. Thus, the states that must balance their budgets annually are faced with the major brunt of the expenses. In most states, incarceration is taking up 20 percent or more of the state's budget. California must release about 15 percent of its prisoners in its quest to balance its budget. Increasingly, America's prisons are overcrowded, becoming more dangerous places both for the guards and inmates. At the present level of incarceration in America, the country is now facing the problem of more resources being dedicated to prison than to education. A central question becomes does America wish to put its men and women in prison and lose this tremendous source of energy and imagination?

Another interesting comparison is that, at the present rate of imprisonment, America now has more prisoners than it has soldiers.

## Where Does This Put America?

There are now over 4,000 federal crimes and many times that number of federal regulations carrying criminal penalties. Recently, analysts at the Congressional Research Service tried to count the number of separate offenses on the books and gave up. Rules concerning corporate governance or the environment are often impossible to understand yet breaking them will land you in jail. In many criminal cases, the common law requirement that a defendant must have a "mens rea" (he must or should know that he is doing wrong) has been virtually eliminated.

The founders of America viewed the criminal sanction as a last resort, reserved for serious offenses, clearly defined, so that ordinary citizens would know that they were violating the law. Yet over the past 40 years, with acceleration in the past 20, an unholy alliance of big-business-hating liberals and tough-on-crime conservatives made criminalization the first line of attack as a way of demonstrating the seriousness of government to cure the social problems of the moment. "Whether it is a corporate scandal or email scam," writes Gene Healy, a libertarian scholar, "you will do the time." A person can serve federal time for interstate transportation of water hyacinths, trafficking in unlicensed dentures, or misappropriating the likeness of Woodsy Owl.

You are a federal criminal if you make a false statement to a federal official or if you lie to someone who then repeats the lie to a federal official. Failing to prevent your employees from breaking regulations you may never have heard of is also a crime. Recently, a manager was sentenced to six months in prison because his employee broke a pipe that caused oil to spill into a river. While such cases are only a small portion of the total, they matter because they shift scare resources from enforcing laws that really protect society.

## Does This New Focus Work?

Does prison deter crime? Most penologists believe America's present system is not working to deter the most grievous offenders. While some crime has fallen in the past decade, it is questionable whether it is a result of the penal system and criminal laws or if it is because of America's prosperity. One scholar, John Donohue, of the Yale Law School, estimated that a 10 percent increase in incarceration only reduces crime by 2 percent. If we take the lock-them-up-and-throw-away-the-key philosophy to its logical conclusion, then America could do away with virtually all crime if, say, 90 percent of its population were to be locked up. Obviously, the society would have lost all meaning of freedom at that point.

Jim Felman, a defense lawyer in Tampa, Florida, says America is conducting "an experiment by imprisoning first-time, non-violent offenders for periods of time previously reserved only for the most serious of offenders, normally for people who had murdered someone." An organization called Lifeforpot found there are seven men in federal prison doing life sentences for first-time, non-violent marijuana offenses. The authors of this book are first-time, non-violent offenders. One has served 24 years of life imprisonment on a marijuana sentence and the other is serving a 20 year sentence for a white collar crime. One is 54 years old and the other is 71 years old. With their sentences, they will languish in prison with a possibility of dying before being released. There are now 6,000 men in the Federal Bureau of Prisons with life sentences, without any possibility of release. With penalties as harsh as they are today, the incentive of the targeted is to cooperate, which means to be helpful to the prosecutors, and this, according to most people close to the system, "warps the truth seeking function of justice."

Innocent defendants, or defendants guilty of a lesser crime, may even plead guilty in return for a shorter sentence in order to avoid the risk of going to trial. A prosecutor can credibly threaten a middle-aged man with the menacing promise that he will die in prison if he doesn't testify against his boss or friend. If a defendant offers a witness money it is bribery but, if a prosecutor offers a witness liberty, it is justice.

Half the states lock up habitual offenders for life. In some states, it is only violent offenders but, in others, it is for all repeat offenders regardless of their prior offenses. In California, some 3,700 people who committed neither violent nor serious crimes are serving life sentences under the "three strikes and you are out laws."

# Jail Is More Expensive

Prison has become more and more costly, with some penologists suggesting that we have passed the point of diminishing returns. A report by the Pew Center states that for each dollar spent on incarceration, less than a dollar of harm will be averted. In 1980, in the state of Washington, each dollar of prison costs averted more than $9 of criminal harm. But by 2001, as the emphasis shifted from violent criminals to drug dealers and thieves, this cost to benefit ratio went to each dollar of prison cost only averted $0.37 worth of harm.

A less punitive system could work better, argues Mark Kleiman of the University of California. Swift and certain lesser sentences work far better than the present system of harsh sentences. Money spent on prison cannot be spent on other more cost-effective systems such as better schooling, counseling for troubled youth, drug prevention and counseling programs, and even probation with supervision. The pain that punishment inflicts on criminals themselves also affects their families and communities. Total impact analysis must be made when considering harsh incarceration and sentencing.

Just by making effective use of things we already have, we could reasonably expect to have half as much crime and half as many people behind bars as we do today. This would mean half as much expense and half as much trauma to family structure. There can be a thousand excuses for failing to make the effort but not one good reason. Incarceration in America today epitomizes the imbalance of resources being misspent, based on half thought-out concepts. Besides all the other sociological and humanitarian reasons, the present American system of incarceration makes no economic sense in a world where we must make even more calculated decisions based on scare resources.

Alternatives to incarceration in prison, such as home confinement or community service, must be considered, especially for first-time, non-violent offenders. The American taxpayers are required to provide healthcare for all prisoners. As the prison population ages, this cost will continue to skyrocket. The thought of many citizens may be "stop giving prisoners healthcare" but this is an unconstitutional alternative. Indeed, prisoners are the only class of citizens with a constitutional guarantee to healthcare.

## *Some Immediate Solutions*

Without redoing a plethora of laws, America can immediately begin to correct the imbalance in its incarceration system by bringing back parole and by beginning to give good time for education, other rehabilitative efforts, and good behavior. What would this do? It would have an effect of dramatically reducing the number of incarcerated while, at the same time, stimulating rehabilitation to prevent inmates from leaving the prison only to return for another offense (the revolving door effect). Presently, there are few incentives for prisoners to truly turn their lives around by rehabilitation. With a return to parole and good time, the whole focus on incarceration would change dramatically and rapidly.

If America were to begin such reform, it could probably reduce its number of incarcerated by one quarter within the first few years to one half within 10 years. This would save $40 to $60 billion annually. Most of this would benefit hard pressed state governments but, even in the federal system, this would amount to several billion dollars saved annually almost immediately.

# CHAPTER XIII

# POPULATION

*"The most incomprehensible thing about the world is that it is comprehensible."*

ALBERT EINSTEIN

*"Grant me chastity and continence, but not yet."*

AUGUSTINUS AURELIUS OF HIPPO (SAINT AUGUSTINE)

*"Each man is the architect of his own fate."*

TIBERIUS CLAUDIUS CAESAR AUGUSTUS GERMANICUS

*"Anyway, I am sure that he (God) does not play dice."*

ALBERT EINSTEIN

In 1798, Thomas Robert Malthus wrote of the ominous laws of population growth in his "Essay on the Principle of Population." In a pithy style, in what was to become known as the "dismal science," Malthus hypothesized that population growth will eventually diminish the ability of the world to feed itself. He said population would grow in such a way as to overtake the possibility of adding enough land for crops to feed the increased population or, in mathematical terms, population growth is geometric while food growth is arithmetic.

An analysis of world population growth lends credence to Malthus' view. It took from the beginning of the world to the early 1800's to reach the first one billion of population. The second billion came in another hundred years and the third billion by 1969. By 1987, the world population reached the fifth billion and, by 1997, it passed six billion. It is projected that world population will pass ten billion by 2080, where some speculate it will stabilize.

Figure 14 shows how population increase has occurred since 1800 to the present.

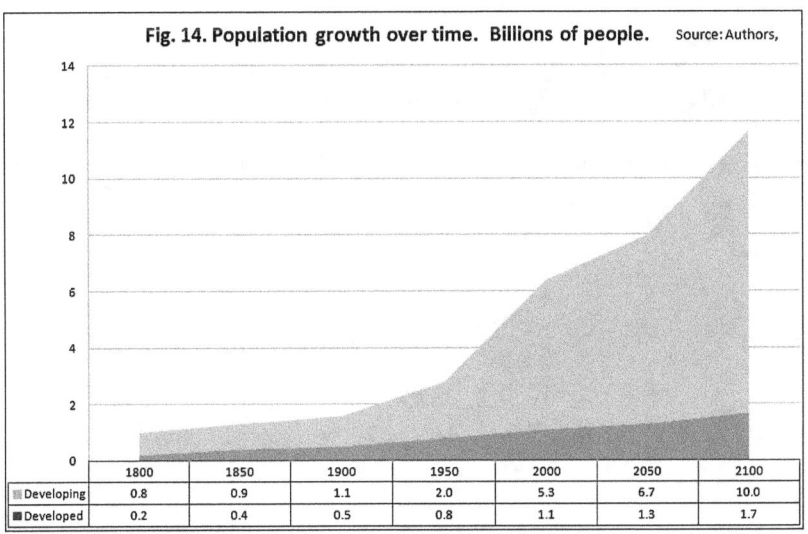

Fig. 14. Population growth over time. Billions of people. Source: Authors,

| | 1800 | 1850 | 1900 | 1950 | 2000 | 2050 | 2100 |
|---|---|---|---|---|---|---|---|
| Developing | 0.8 | 0.9 | 1.1 | 2.0 | 5.3 | 6.7 | 10.0 |
| Developed | 0.2 | 0.4 | 0.5 | 0.8 | 1.1 | 1.3 | 1.7 |

This shows the dramatic population shift that is occurring from the developed world to the developing world. It also is a validation of the Malthusian theory of geometric population growth, especially beginning in the 20th century.

In simple economic terms, the formula for population growth is $N = B + I - D - E$, or population change to a country comes by adding births and immigration and deducting deaths and emigration. In this regard, it must be observed that the most significant change in the past century has been the increase of life expectancy, by better medicine and better diets. But accompanying this has been a significant decrease of birth rates in the developed nations. This combination has led to the phenomenon of world population shifting more and more to the developing nations. Indeed, in some European nations, there is actually a negative growth rate due to the decline in births.

The Figures 15, 16, and 17 illustrate this shift dramatically.

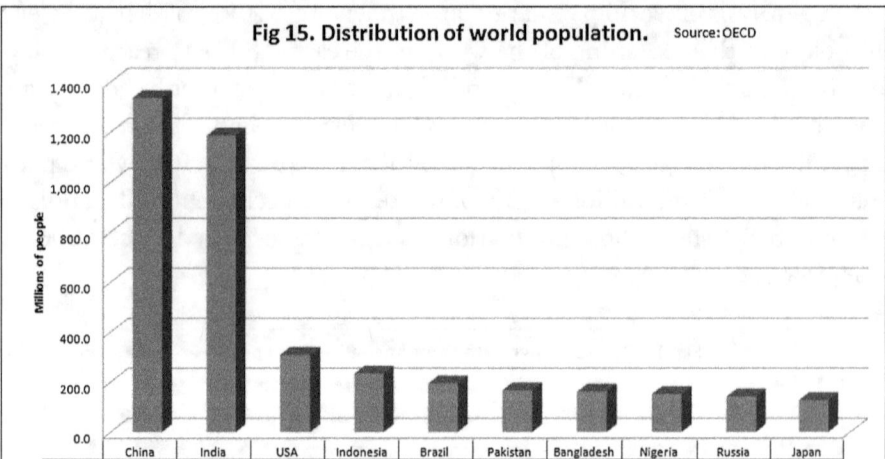

Fig 15. Distribution of world population. Source: OECD

| Country | China | India | USA | Indonesia | Brazil | Pakistan | Bangladesh | Nigeria | Russia | Japan |
|---|---|---|---|---|---|---|---|---|---|---|
| Country | 1,336.3 | 1,186.2 | 308.8 | 234.0 | 194.2 | 167.0 | 161.3 | 151.5 | 141.8 | 127.9 |

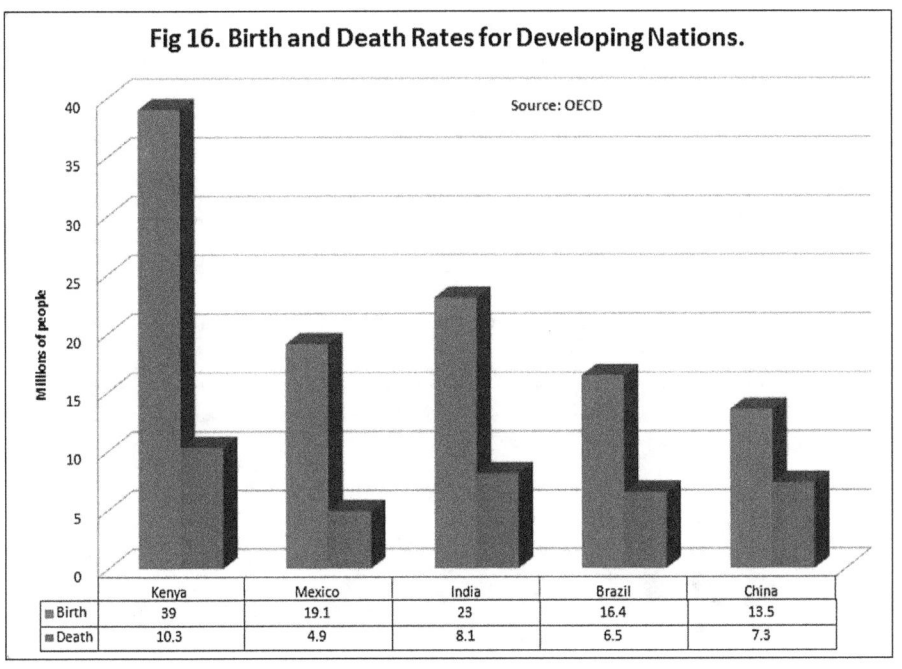

Fig 16. Birth and Death Rates for Developing Nations.

Source: OECD

| | Kenya | Mexico | India | Brazil | China |
|---|---|---|---|---|---|
| Birth | 39 | 19.1 | 23 | 16.4 | 13.5 |
| Death | 10.3 | 4.9 | 8.1 | 6.5 | 7.3 |

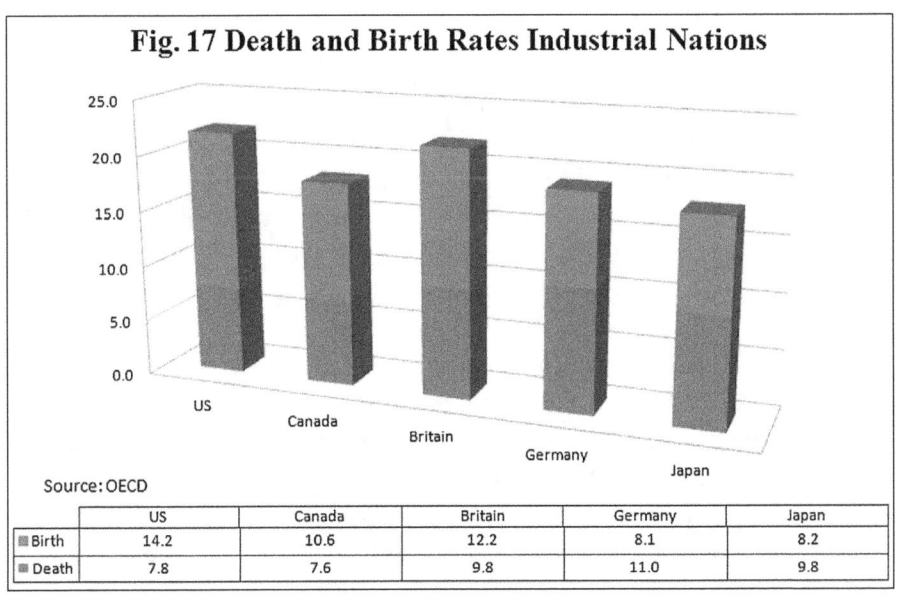

Fig. 17 Death and Birth Rates Industrial Nations

Source: OECD

| | US | Canada | Britain | Germany | Japan |
|---|---|---|---|---|---|
| Birth | 14.2 | 10.6 | 12.2 | 8.1 | 8.2 |
| Death | 7.8 | 7.6 | 9.8 | 11.0 | 9.8 |

To see where the world is and where it is going, the population numbers must be analyzed. The following chart shows that one third of world population presently is in two countries, India and China. But most significantly, countries such as Indonesia, Brazil, Pakistan and Bangladesh occupy the 5th, 6th, 7th and 8th positions and are growing, population-wise, at a rate over 30 percent more than most of the developed world. In this regard, it should be noted that, the combination of the European countries of Germany, France, Italy and Britain were about 260 million in 2007, about the size Indonesia is projected to be in 2025.

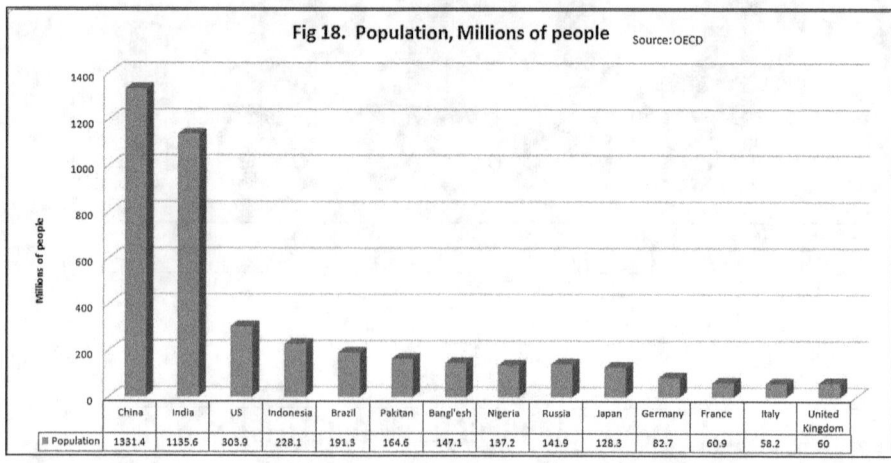

Fig 18. Population, Millions of people    Source: OECD

| | China | India | US | Indonesia | Brazil | Pakitan | Bangl'esh | Nigeria | Russia | Japan | Germany | France | Italy | United Kingdom |
|---|---|---|---|---|---|---|---|---|---|---|---|---|---|---|
| Population | 1331.4 | 1135.6 | 303.9 | 228.1 | 191.3 | 164.6 | 147.1 | 137.2 | 141.9 | 128.3 | 82.7 | 60.9 | 58.2 | 60 |

By the 1990's, nearly 60 percent of the world's population lived in Asia. Europe, excluding Russia, had 10 percent and North, Central, and South America had 13 percent. The most densely populated continent was Asia, with about 296 persons per square mile. Europe, including Russia, had 183 and North America had 39. Bangladesh has the greatest density with other population dense countries being Taiwan, South Korea, the Netherlands, Belgium, and Japan.

A nation's age-structure influences how that population lives and how its resources are allocated. Developing countries have a much higher proportion of their populations in children under the age of 15, which can run as high as 45 percent of their populations. This compares with developed countries where Sweden, for example, has only 18 percent of its population less than 15 years old. This requires a greater expenditure on education in developing counties. The opposite is that developed countries, with a higher percentage of their populations over 60 years of age, have to use a greater percentage of resources to support their older citizens. This is especially significant in health care, where age-related infirmities can consume more than 80 percent of a person's life-time health expenses. This phenomenon has caused serious debate concerning the allocation of health care expenditures to older people during the recent health insurance debates in the U.S.

Much of the increases in population size, in the developing countries, are in urban areas. The proportions up through 1990 were 37 percent of total population living in urban centers in developing countries while almost 73 percent of the populations of developed countries lived in urban settings. By 2010, this overall percentage changed to about 50 percent of the world's population being urban. Of the major cities, five cities in the developing world have more than 15 million in population: Mexico City, Shanghai, Sao Paulo, Calcutta and Bombay. The developed world had two such cities: Tokyo and New York. This increased urbanization requires a new focus in urban job creation, education, and other supporting services.

In the United States during the 1980's, more than 25 percent of the growth of population came from immigration. By the 1990's, largely due to an unexpected rise in birthrate, the increase from immigration dropped to less than 15 percent. Significantly, these figures did not include the undocumented aliens who migrated to the United States.

In spite of the temporary increase in birthrates, the United States is becoming a nation with a population shifting to older people, much like Europe and Japan. At the beginning of the 20th century, the U.S. had 34 percent of its population in children under 15. By the early, 1990's, less than 22 percent were children under 15.

The number of retired people has also increased faster than the number of productive workers (aged 18 to 64). With baby boomers (people born between 1946 and 1964), this shift is accelerating. This means that one of several things will have to occur: either a reshaping of Social Security relative to when benefits occur, an increase in the Social Security tax rate, or a significant increase in productivity. Probably some combination will happen.

Significantly, the U.S. is projected to continue to be among the most rapidly growing of the world's countries, in part because of immigration. The increased size of the Hispanic population combined with the African American minority's size will place the two together as a majority within the next ten years. This will have significant political and economic effects in everything from voting to economic activity such as consumption, wages, and investment. For one thing, it is difficult to imagine what the Southwest agriculture sector would do for picking and harvesting such food products as lettuce and tomatoes, or oranges and other citrus without Mexican labor. On the other hand, the technology and medical sectors are using some highly trained immigrants to supplement native-born Americans. Leading American speakers on the subject such as Mayor Michael Bloomberg of New York and Bill Gates of Microsoft have said it would be a net negative to America to diminish this brain power migration to the U.S.

## Future Prospects

Clearly, increases in population augments demand for limited resources such as environmental resources of clean air, arable land, and potable water but also educational services, infrastructure, and the technologies that go with them. The question becomes whether and how these services are increased to meet rising population demands through invention, discovery, and research. In great part, the answer to that question depends on where and how the population increases occur and on the political and social will of the country and people involved.

For the world at large, the United States, and the other faster growing countries in particular, the socio-economic, human issue is whether family size in places where opportunities and resources are scarce should be limited by government policy. The two population giants, China and India, have taken opposite approaches to this. China has restricted the number of offspring born to a family as a matter of law, while India has absolutely no restrictions. These policies are already showing dramatic results. China stabilized its population and its resources are catching up with its size, while population in India just keeps on growing. In the United States, population growth through illegal immigration has become a major political issue as the number of undocumented immigrants has swelled to over 12 million as of 2010. On one hand, supporting services have been strained in many states in the U.S. with heavy illegal immigrant populations. On the other hand, unskilled labor industries such as agriculture, hotels, and construction have benefited by the lower paid immigrant labor that appears willing to work at many tasks, and for wages, most Americans would not do. In decreasing population countries such as Germany and France, the opposite approach has been taken: bring in documented "guest workers" to do the menial but necessary jobs most Germans, or French simply do not want to do.

So this complex but pertinent problem of the 21ˢᵗ century has two aspects: 1) from an economic point of view, can the expected benefits to society of a growing population outweigh the expected and more easily quantifiable, estimated socio-economic costs and 2) from a moral point of view, what should governments do in terms of either promoting or restricting population changes. These two facets pose especially poignant problems to the United States, a country built on large immigration waves.

Nonetheless, the question exists and must be answered. It comes down to utilization of scarce resources. These problems must be answered in an intelligent and planned discussion on how to manage our resources to accommodate the ever increasing U.S. population.

## Population in the United States in the 21ˢᵗ Century

The United States has benefited from population growth in excess of other developed countries during most of the 20ᵗʰ century. Both the baby boomers and the influx of undocumented from Mexico and Central America have expanded the population and probably accounted for at least 1 to 1.5 percent of annual GDP increases in the last 30 years of the 20ᵗʰ century. Even with the increases in productivity, which averaged about 1.7 percent annually since 1960 with declining population, increases in GDP growth could fall to 2.2 percent from the historic level of 3.3 percent annually.

In other words, the fertility decline that accompanies modernity will directly impact the United States in the 21ˢᵗ century. With an estimated 12 million undocumented immigrants in the United States as of the end of the 20th Century, rather than looking to deport them, some type of accommodation that allows them to remain and earn citizenship makes more economic sense. These immigrants continue to add to the national economy by working at lower paying, more labor-intense jobs. A guest worker program with work visas allowing for eventual citizenship would be one solution.

However, in order to meet the needs of an economy which will be ever more high technology/information processing oriented, the United

States will have to raise the level of education and attract highly skilled immigrants. Presently, visa programs exist in the U.S. for such skilled immigrants. Also, the U.S.' university traditionally attracts foreign-born individuals, many of whom choose to remain in the U.S. after completing their U.S. university training. Both visa programs and stimuli to attract foreign-born, U.S. university-trained people should be expanded.

# CHAPTER XIV

# CURRENCY

*"Lenin was certainly right. There is no subtler, no surer means of overturning the existing basis of society than to debauch the currency. The process engages all the hidden forces of economic law on the side of destruction, and does it in a manner which not one man in a million is able to diagnose."*

JOHN MAYNARD KEYNES

*"Much discussion of money involves a heavy incantation of priestly incantation."*

JOHN KENNETH GALBRAITH

*"He that will write well in any tongue, must follow the counsel of Aristotle, to speak as the common people do, to think as the wise men do; and so should every man understand him, and the judgment of wise allow him."*

ROGER ASCHAM

The United States came out of World Wars I and II as the world's dominant power. Going into the 20<sup>th</sup> century, through the Great Depression years, the world was on a gold standard. This required that currencies have gold backing. It had the advantage of acting as a brake on uncontrolled monetary expansion and the disadvantage of limiting the money supply to a finite number equal to the amount of gold a country had in its reserves. Immediately following World War I, there was extreme volatility and high speculation in foreign exchange. After the Great Depression and the suspension of the gold standard in 1933, the developed countries of the world were in an unstable state with a system of floating exchange rates. In 1944, the allies (the United States, Great Britain and France) met at the United Nations Monetary Financial Conference in Bretton Woods, New Hampshire. Out of Bretton Woods, two things developed: the pegging of currencies and the International Monetary Fund (IMF). The major trading currencies were pegged to the U.S. dollar and only allowed to fluctuate one percent on either side of that rate. When a currency exceeded that range, the central bank in charge had to buy or sell it, thus bringing it back into range. In turn, the U.S. dollar was pegged to gold at $35 per ounce. This made the U.S. dollar the world's reserve currency and guaranteed the U.S.'s place as the world's economic superpower.

A period of relative currency stability up to the time of the Korean and Vietnam wars followed when secular inflation occurred with price levels going up three times. Consequently, gold became very undervalued and European countries traded in dollars for gold until the U.S. lost more than half of its stock. In 1971, under President Richard Nixon, the U.S. no longer guaranteed the price of gold at $35 per ounce with the backing of dollars by gold reserves. This began the breakdown of the fixed exchange rate system of Bretton Woods. There was no longer any mechanism to keep the world price levels in line with the price of gold.

## Bretton Woods

The emulated, fixed-exchange rate system of Bretton Woods served several purposes. It helped to avoid the stop-and-go situation of the inter-war period when governments resorted to floating exchange rates while under economic pressure. Most importantly, it afforded a nurturing environment much needed by the world to enable the crippled nations to rebuild themselves. The world saw most of its industrial infrastructure destroyed. There was major social disruption and the political balance that existed before the war was totally distorted. Following the wars, there were few stable and strong currencies besides the dollar. So the world needed the secure and protective setting of Bretton Woods and a system fixed to the dollar. This required the actions of the central banks to maintain the intervention points. Also, there had to be a continuous and common effort to bring the various parties together into long term stable relationships.

Thus, the United States, out of world necessity, became the central link to stabilizing and rebuilding a badly damaged world. The dollar, in turn, became the world's reserve currency, substituting the place played by gold prior to the war. This put tremendous responsibility on the U.S. but also gave it a very real advantage. All trade and development was skewed to the U.S. out of necessity in the new structure and with the institutions created by Bretton Woods.

While it was far from perfect, the Bretton Woods Accord lasted 27 years, from 1944 through 1971. Under its auspices, a broken Japan and Germany were able to reinvent themselves. However, from its inception, it was largely a one nation show. Once recovered, both Japan and Germany began to offer competition within the dollar block. It became apparent that the U.S. gained more than the other nations and was, in effect, exporting inflation. The artificially created ranges outlived their usefulness and the rates of growth and rates of inflation among the major economies were widening. There followed a number of programs to switch from the Bretton Woods fixed exchange rate system.

## Post Bretton Woods

Initially, there was the Smithsonian Agreement of December 1971 in which ranges were from 1 percent to 4.5 percent against the U.S. dollar. Against each other, the currencies could fluctuate as much as 9 percent.

Parallel to this effort, the European Economic Community was established in 1957 and attempted to move from the U.S. dollar to the Deutsche mark. The European Joint Float was established in April 1972 between West Germany, France, Italy, the Netherlands, Belgium and Luxembourg. The member countries were allowed to have their currencies fluctuate against the U.S. dollar within a 2.25 percent band, known as the snake.

Unfortunately, neither agreement focused on the independent domestic problems from the bottom up. Instead, focus was on the larger international picture with attempts to solve the international monetary situation by artificially enforced intervention points. By 1973, both failed.

But the idea of regional currency stability and financial independence from the U.S. dollar persisted and the European Economic Community launched a revamped European Joint Float in March 1979 with such features as the threshold of divergence. This lasted until 1993 when the collapse of Communism began to set off a series of economic imbalances that couldn't be fixed by means of intervention points.

The double demise of the Smithsonian Agreement and the European Joint Float in 1973 began a period of free-floating, foreign exchange markets. This was by default and was not imposed. In other words, countries were free to peg, semi peg, or free float their currencies.

## Currency Reserves

Countries will hold a part of their wealth in currencies or commodities perceived as safe havens. Additionally, many international transactions will be executed in currencies other than domestic ones. These are called reserve currencies. Usually the dominant world power has its currency recognized as the reserve currency. Prior to World War II, it was the British pound and since then it has been the U.S. dollar.

By the end of 2004, two thirds of official foreign reserves were held in dollars and about one quarter was held in the new Euro. Most of the remainder was held in British pounds. China and Japan, as two of the largest export countries, held the largest foreign exchange reserves, in excess of $1.5 trillion for the dollar and in excess of $1 trillion for the pound by 2009. Other nations with large trade surpluses such as Russia, Taiwan, and South Korea also have large dollar foreign exchange reserves.

In the 21$^{st}$ century, the trend will be for medium and small central banks to diversify away from dollars and into other currencies, primarily Euros, but also pound sterling. There will be a movement to craft a mixed basket of currencies. Oil exporters, such as Qatar and Iraq before the fall of Saddam Hussein, planned to price their oil exports in such a basket of currencies.

Such a movement away from the dollar is both a political reality of a new world in which the U.S.'s total domination begins to wane and the economic reality of a world in which other currencies have equal or greater stability and less devaluation through inflation than the U.S.

## European Monetary Union and the Euro

The new European currency of the euro was launched in January 1999. This followed the formation of the European Monetary Union (EMU) in 1979 with the seven European capitalist countries of West Germany, France, the Netherlands, Belgium, Luxembourg, Denmark, and Ireland. Great Britain and Italy joined under special conditions but Britain never voted to adopt the euro as its currency. Greece joined in 1981 then Spain and Portugal in 1986 with Britain only joining the Exchange Rate Mechanism (ERM) in 1990.

Since its formation, other European countries have joined the European Common Market (ECM) including Cyprus, the Czech Republic, Estonia, Hungary, Latvia, Lithuania, Malta, Poland, Slovakia, and Slovenia in 2004.

As of 2006, nations with more than 457 million people were members of the ECM and used the euro as their currency. Their combined GDP now exceeds that of the U.S. It offers an alternative to the power of the U.S., China, or Japan as an economic bloc.

The ECM requires its members to adhere to a set of economic standards. These include a maximum allowable fiscal deficit of 3 percent of GDP among other political and economic conditions which must be maintained by members. Recent crises caused by the world economic meltdown of 2008-09 have exasperated the economics of several ECM countries, namely Portugal, Greece, Ireland, and Spain and have required major bailouts by other members. This has led to the questioning of the very sustainability of the European Economic Union and the euro.

Overall, the European Economic Union has stimulated trade between the member nations by offering a common currency other than the dollar, by virtually eliminating tariff barriers between the countries, and by standardizing and controlling major economic policies. In addition to the euro's utilization by the trading members, it has increasingly become an alternative currency of reserve and trade in substitute for the dollar by other countries throughout the world.

## World Trade

In 2007, world trade was dominated by the Euro block countries, the United States and China.

However, when analyzing the following figures, surpluses and deficits must be focused on. This means that a country must be analyzed not just for exports but also for imports to see if the net result is positive or negative. A country can have a temporary imbalance in its current accounts but must bring these this into balance. See Figures 19, 20, 21a, 21b.

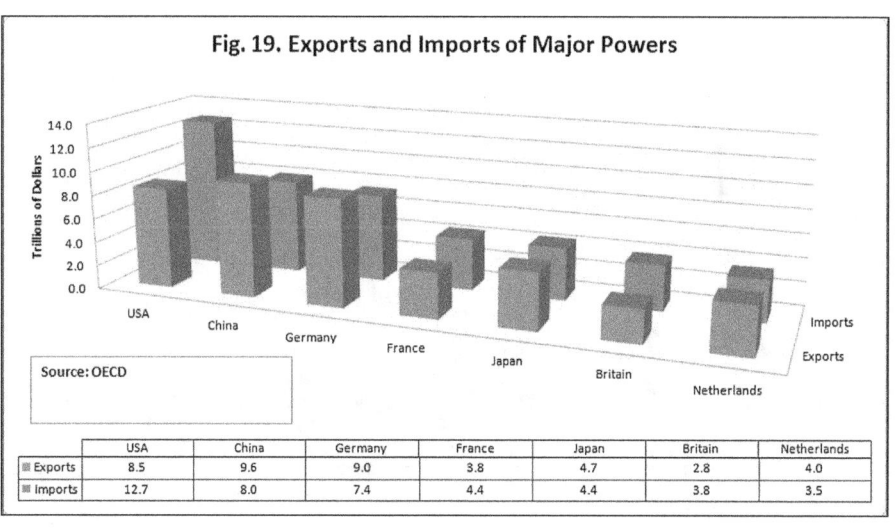

Fig. 19. Exports and Imports of Major Powers

Source: OECD

|  | USA | China | Germany | France | Japan | Britain | Netherlands |
|---|---|---|---|---|---|---|---|
| Exports | 8.5 | 9.6 | 9.0 | 3.8 | 4.7 | 2.8 | 4.0 |
| Imports | 12.7 | 8.0 | 7.4 | 4.4 | 4.4 | 3.8 | 3.5 |

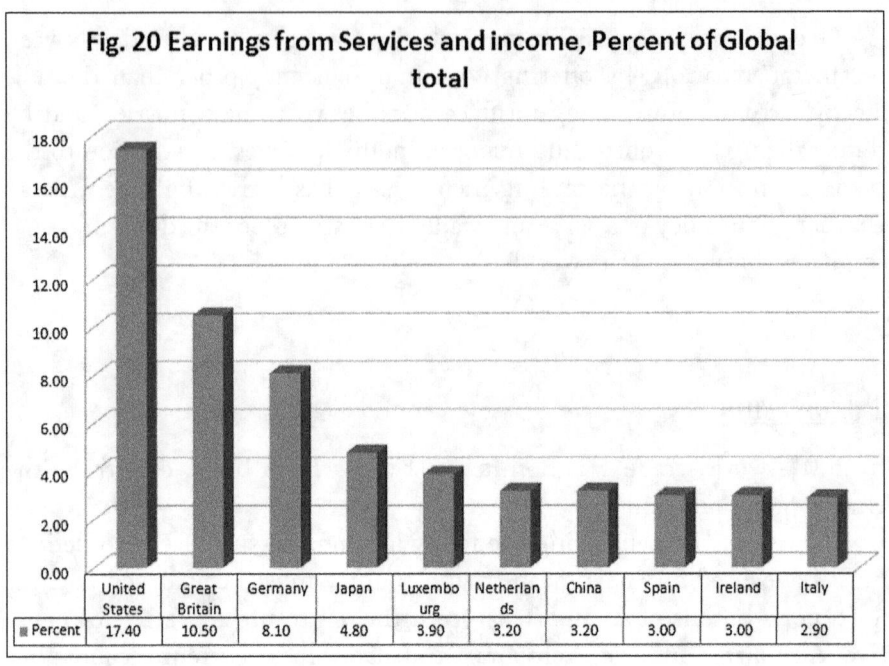

Fig. 20 Earnings from Services and income, Percent of Global total

| | United States | Great Britain | Germany | Japan | Luxembo urg | Netherlan ds | China | Spain | Ireland | Italy |
|---|---|---|---|---|---|---|---|---|---|---|
| Percent | 17.40 | 10.50 | 8.10 | 4.80 | 3.90 | 3.20 | 3.20 | 3.00 | 3.00 | 2.90 |

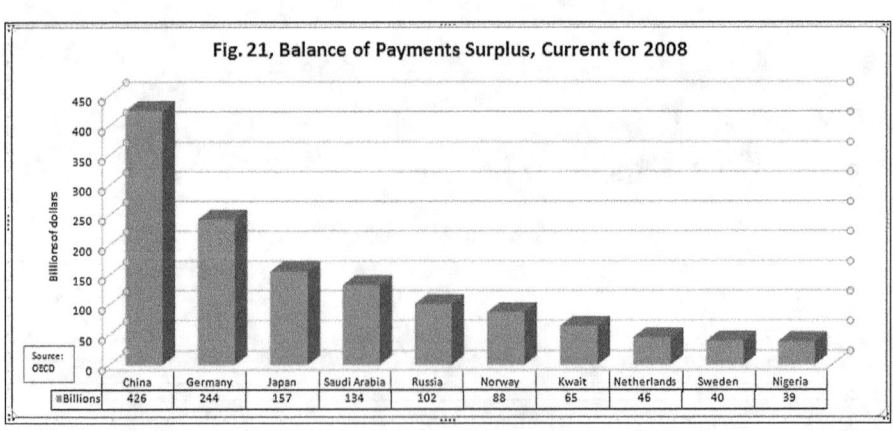

Fig. 21, Balance of Payments Surplus, Current for 2008

Billions of dollars

Source: OECD

| | China | Germany | Japan | Saudi Arabia | Russia | Norway | Kwait | Netherlands | Sweden | Nigeria |
|---|---|---|---|---|---|---|---|---|---|---|
| Billions | 426 | 244 | 157 | 134 | 102 | 88 | 65 | 46 | 40 | 39 |

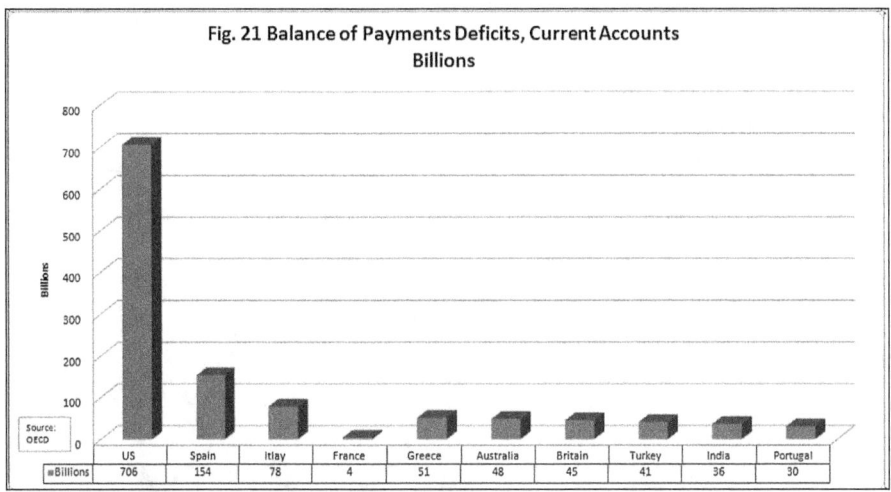

Fig. 21 Balance of Payments Deficits, Current Accounts
Billions

| | US | Spain | Itlay | France | Greece | Australia | Britain | Turkey | India | Portugal |
|---|---|---|---|---|---|---|---|---|---|---|
| ■Billions | 706 | 154 | 78 | 4 | 51 | 48 | 45 | 41 | 36 | 30 |

The United States is the country with the largest trade imbalance because it imports significantly more than its exports. China, Germany and
Japan have positive trade balances because they export significantly more
than they import.

This has resulted in the official reserve position of these exporting
countries increasing. See following Figures 22 and 23.

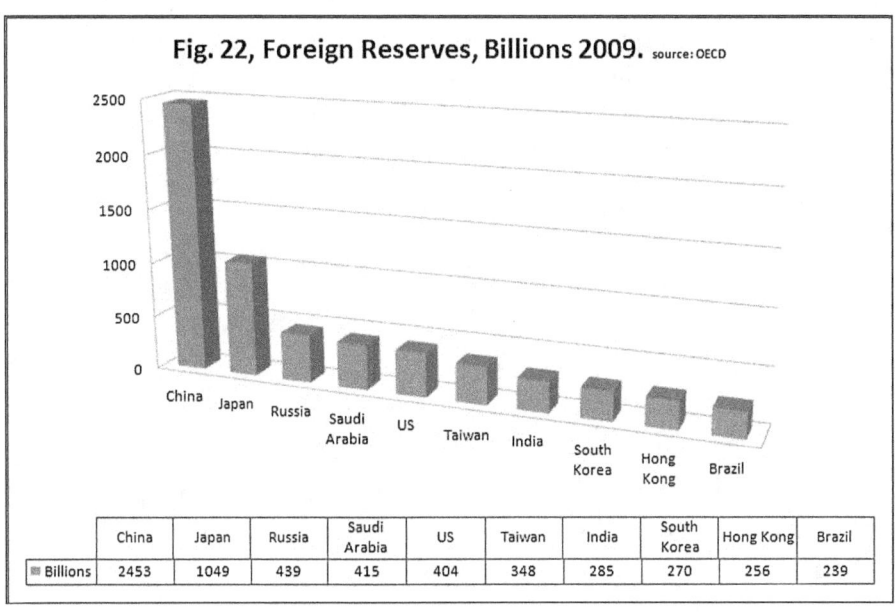

Fig. 22, Foreign Reserves, Billions 2009. source: OECD

| | China | Japan | Russia | Saudi Arabia | US | Taiwan | India | South Korea | Hong Kong | Brazil |
|---|---|---|---|---|---|---|---|---|---|---|
| ■ Billions | 2453 | 1049 | 439 | 415 | 404 | 348 | 285 | 270 | 256 | 239 |

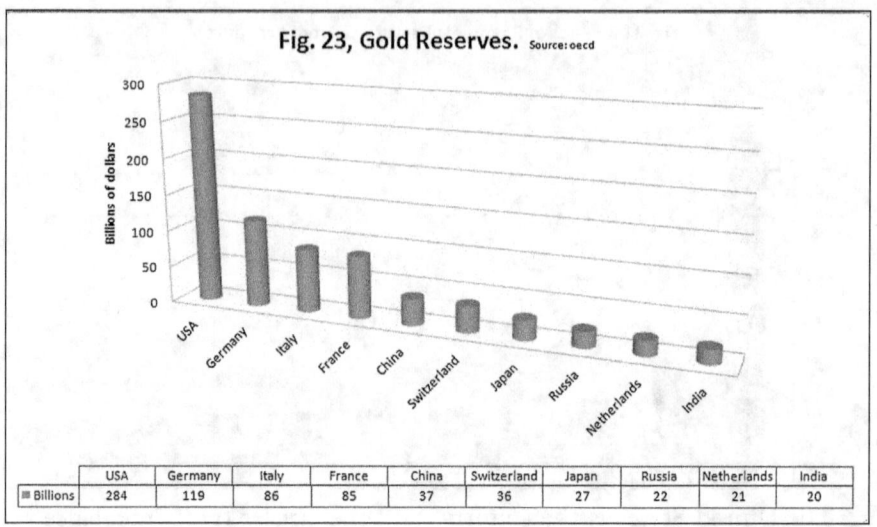

Fig. 23, Gold Reserves. Source: oecd

| | USA | Germany | Italy | France | China | Switzerland | Japan | Russia | Netherlands | India |
|---|---|---|---|---|---|---|---|---|---|---|
| ≡ Billions | 284 | 119 | 86 | 85 | 37 | 36 | 27 | 22 | 21 | 20 |

Analyzing these figures, we see that China, Japan, Russia, and the Euro area countries had combined reserves of over $3.5 trillion in 2007. The U.S., India, Taiwan and South Korea -the next 4 largest nations - had combined reserves of about $1 trillion. These 8 nations have more than 60 percent of the world's foreign currency reserves. Significantly, the U.S. dollar represented about 52 percent of these total reserves with the euro making up about 22 percent, the Japanese yen another 12 percent, the British pound about 10 percent and the Swiss franc about 4 percent.

The trade balances of the major trading nations of the world broke down in 2008 as shown in Figures 24 and 25.

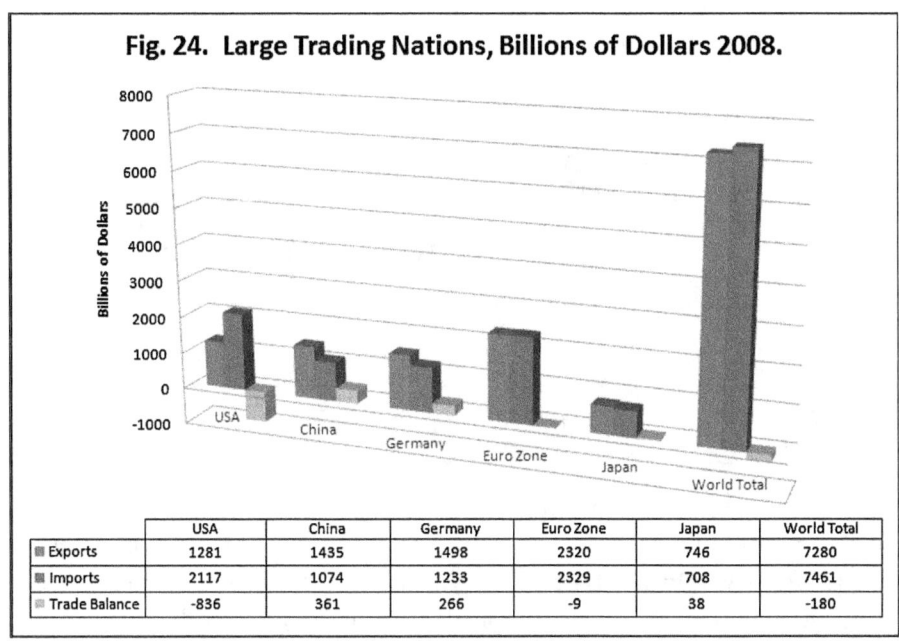

**Fig. 24. Large Trading Nations, Billions of Dollars 2008.**

|  | USA | China | Germany | Euro Zone | Japan | World Total |
|---|---|---|---|---|---|---|
| Exports | 1281 | 1435 | 1498 | 2320 | 746 | 7280 |
| Imports | 2117 | 1074 | 1233 | 2329 | 708 | 7461 |
| Trade Balance | -836 | 361 | 266 | -9 | 38 | -180 |

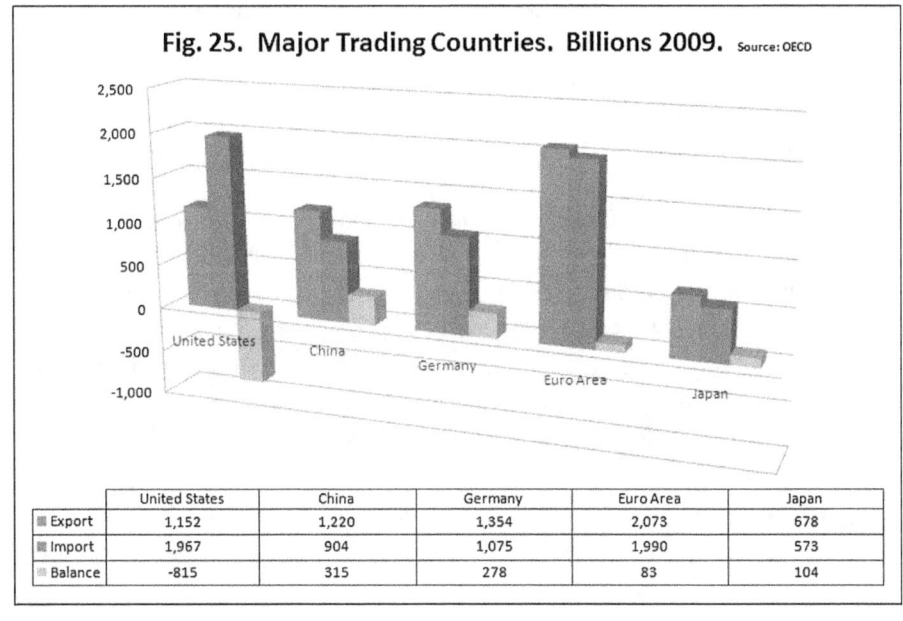

**Fig. 25. Major Trading Countries. Billions 2009.** Source: OECD

|  | United States | China | Germany | Euro Area | Japan |
|---|---|---|---|---|---|
| Export | 1,152 | 1,220 | 1,354 | 2,073 | 678 |
| Import | 1,967 | 904 | 1,075 | 1,990 | 573 |
| Balance | -815 | 315 | 278 | 83 | 104 |

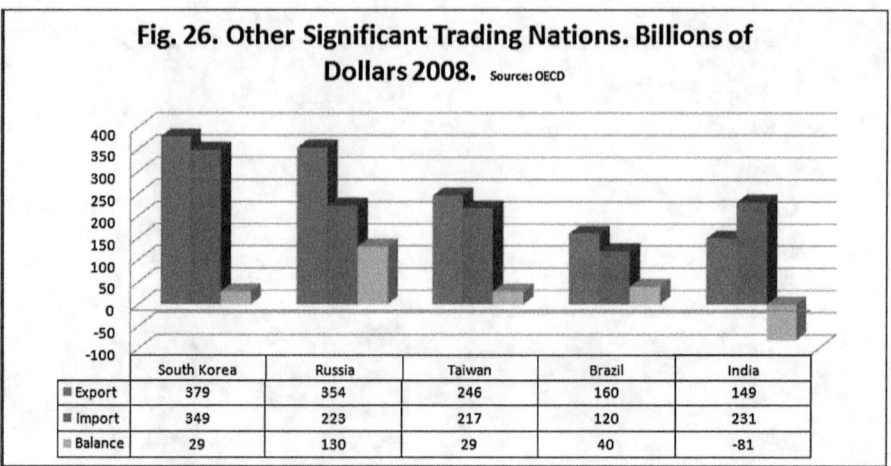

Fig. 26. Other Significant Trading Nations. Billions of Dollars 2008. Source: OECD

| | South Korea | Russia | Taiwan | Brazil | India |
|---|---|---|---|---|---|
| ■ Export | 379 | 354 | 246 | 160 | 149 |
| ■ Import | 349 | 223 | 217 | 120 | 231 |
| ■ Balance | 29 | 130 | 29 | 40 | -81 |

As seen, the U.S. is the odd boy on the block with a huge trade deficit. Without the dominant position of the dollar as the world reserve currency, this position would not be tenable. In essence, the U.S. is living on borrowed money to purchase goods and services it could not otherwise afford. Only because of this current account deficit was the U.S. able to borrow enough money from its trading partners to finance its fiscal deficit.

## Percent of Budget

Presently, interest on Treasury bonds runs to approximately 7 percent of the federal budget. With its high credit rating, the U.S. has been able to finance this debt at relatively low interest rates. However, at the present unsustainable level of fiscal deficits, this now is about 10 percent of GDP. It will be increasingly difficult for the U.S. to continue to borrow at such low rates. Its credit rating has fallen again, resulting in much higher interest payments on Treasury debt. Office of Management and Budget projections show that continuing federal deficits and increasing interest rates could raise such payments to more than 40 percent of the federal budget in 20 years. The 2010 examples of the European countries of Greece, Spain, and Ireland show what happens when a country's fiscal policy is judged profligate by the international community.

# World Unrest with Dollar as Reserve Currency

The underlying truth concerning today's international currency system is that no one is happy with it. No one is satisfied with the current set of rules, norms, and institutions that govern the world currencies and the flow of capital across the border.

There are three broad complaints. First is the complaint concerning the dominance of the dollar as the reserve currency and of America's management of it. The bulk of foreign exchange transactions and reserves are in dollars, even though the U.S. only accounts for 24 percent of global GDP. Most countries believe this dominance in commerce, in commodity pricing, and in official reserves does not reflect the reality of the world economy and leaves the rest of the world vulnerable to America's domestic monetary policy. Second, this has created a vast foreign exchange system. Global reserves have risen from $1.3 trillion (5 percent of world GDP) in 1995 to $8.4 trillion (14 percent) in 2010. Of the total, emerging nations hold two-thirds of the dollar reserves with most of the accumulation in the past ten years. Third, the present system has created a huge scale and volatility of capital flows. This has fomented financial crisis in which emerging countries have suffered floods of capital, as is happening now, and droughts, as happened in 1997-98 and 2008.

# Actual Functioning of System Presently

Any international monetary system is constrained by the "trilemma" of international economics. With capital flowing across the borders, countries must choose between fixing their currencies and controlling their domestic monetary conditions. The simple truth is that they cannot do both. Past experience suggests collapse when countries would not subordinate their domestic policies to an outside link, such as with America and gold in 1971. With no ties to gold or other anchor, today's system has a variety of exchange rate regimes and capital controls. The richer countries' currencies float relatively freely and capital controls have been largely abolished. This has enabled a freer flow of capital to emerging nations. Net flows to these countries have increased from $81 billion annually a decade ago to over $340 billion in 2010.

In today's international currency system, the level of reserves held has expanded greatly. In the 1990's, the rule was for a country to have reserves equal to about 25 percent of GDP or enough to cover a year's worth of debt obligations. Today, most countries far exceed this rule. In fact, China plays the most important role in global monetary system. It has accumulated huge reserves of dollars while keeping its yuan cheap without causing domestic inflation. Many other developing countries have emulated this and a series of dollar shadow countries have developed among the most vibrant of the world's economies, a condition dubbed as "Bretton Woods 2."

## Fear of Trauma Under Present System

Robert Triffen, the Belgian economist, wrote of a tension between emerging economies, their demand for reserves, and their fear that the dollar may lose value. This reliance on a single reserve currency causes the home country to issue assets such as government bonds to lubricate global commerce and meet reserve demand. In the end, there is likelihood the country will not be able to honor its debts. The insatiable appetite for risk-free reserve assets will cause that asset to be anything but risk-free. At the present rates of reserve accumulation, the total of global reserves will rise from about 60 percent of America's GDP today to about 200 percent by 2020 and as high as 700 percent by 2025.

Triffen suggested the solution to this untenable system is to create an artificial reserve asset, tied to a basket of commodities. John Maynard Keynes suggested a similar solution nearly 60 years ago. The Special Drawing Rights (SDR's) of the IMF has emerged, tied to a basket of dollars, yen, pound, and euro but should be revised for a very different world today. For one thing, for the SDR's to become the asset of international reserves, it would have to become much more plentiful (presently about $700 billion annually). Also, it would need deep private markets and would need to be developed with free trading. An alternative to the SDR is the euro as the international reserve currency. Also, China might create an alternative if it allows its yuan to be used for transactions aboard. Probably the most feasible system would be a combination of the SDR with the yuan.

When America's economy improves and its medium-term fiscal outlook improves, the present frantic flow of capital to the emerging economies will also slow. If China makes its yuan more flexible and its capital accounts more open, the international monetary system as it exists will be better able to maintain itself. But, if these two things do not happen, the present, rigid, monetary system will inevitably buckle. Even with the two biggest economies adjusting to the exigencies of a world in which emerging economies are developing with such speed, we will need a revised international monetary system. It isn't whether the system will develop but rather when and in what form. It will behoove the United States to lead in the creation of such a new system.

# EPILOGUE

A s the United States enters this new century, it will need to develop
and implement a new paradigm concerning its socio-economic
structure. The past century was an American century, but no longer do the
same conditions apply. The world is an increasingly complex combination
of equal nations. No longer can it be said that the United States enjoys the
exclusionary position in which its currency, the dollar, is the world's reserve
currency and the only currency of international trade. No longer can it
be said that the United States has the responsibility of being the world's
policeman. No longer can the United States function with an ongoing
trade deficit. No longer can the United States run a fiscal deficit in its
local governance, in its corporate and private citizenry existences and, most
importantly, in its federal government. No longer can the United States
expect the rest of the world to subsidize its excesses, such as the housing
bubble, the financial bubble, and the internet stock bubble all experienced
in the past century. No longer can the United States rest on its laurels as the
technological leader of the world without serious changes in its educational
and research and development structures.

The concluding years of the 20th century and the first decade of the 21st
century, were years in which the United States suffered a major economic
retrenchment. This Great Recession, the most significant such economic
adjustment the United States has had since the Great Depression of 1929-
32, was not a simple cyclical adjustment but rather a major indication of
structural malaise. Institutions have to be rethought and reshaped. The
position of the United States in the community of nations has to be refo-
cused. Many of the basic habits of the United States as to credit, borrowing,

investment, and savings have to be remolded to fit the new century and the new international reality.

To begin with, a major structuring of the fiscal philosophy of the United States is required. No longer can the United States spend recklessly beyond its means. Federal budgets must be made that do not excessively exceed the income from taxation the government receives. Federal planning will require a new austerity that has largely been lost in the past 30 years. When bills are passed by Congress, there must be a focus on how they are paid for and their long-term effects. In other words, lawmakers must take actions that are more than short term politically expedient.

Such austerity measures will probably cause hardships in the short term but will alleviate the longer-term, negative course the United States is now on. Without new focus, it is inevitable that the world financial markets will eventually cause adjustments. The sovereign debt of the United States will be questioned and downgraded resulting in rising interest rates. Presently, even at relatively low interest rates, the debt burden of the United States is approaching difficult levels and will, in a few years, be at dangerous heights.

A major economic macro-focus should be on individual consumption and savings. Americans will have to be weaned off their consumption splurge of the past 30 years that has resulted in an economy in which consumption amounts to 70 percent of GDP. Rather than relying on other nations to lend money to the United States, Americans must again become savers and thus self finance the investments required to grow the economy. From being a negative net saver, the average American must become a positive net saver. Rather than a negative 5 percent of income saved, the average American must become a positive saver of 5 percent or more of his income, such as the average Japanese. This change does appear to be underway.

On the other side of the equation are the taxes Americans pay. Presently, the Congressional Research Service estimates that corporations are paying an effective rate of about 26 percent which is about 4.8 percent of GDP while individual income taxes account for about 8.3 percent of GDP. It is estimated there are over a trillion dollars in tax loopholes that most experts believe should be eliminated. That would, more than anything else, balance the federal budget. Studies in other higher taxation countries show that citizens are willing to pay more taxes when they feel they are getting good services from their tax payments. Tax reform must be implemented in order to simplify an American system that has gotten overly complicated. In such a revised system, there must be an approach of raising the total taxes paid but in an equitable fashion. Most high income people in the United States, studies have shown, are not opposed to paying more taxes and, in all probability, most middle class Americans would not oppose some tax increase if it was clearly shown that such an increase was for the good of the country and supported well-managed programs.

It is beyond any intelligent discussion that there must be serious study given to cutting spending in the three major budgetary areas of Social Security, Medicare and Medicaid, and defense spending. Social Security will have to be overhauled with fixes in age of entitlement and benefits paid. Health care is much more difficult and will probably require some additional funding, although long-term preventative medical systems as well as changes in insurance reform as passed by the Obama administration will be required. Defense spending will have to be approached head-on with the aim of radically different approaches than presently being pursued. Many experts believe the U.S. can achieve national defense objectives while greatly reducing spending.

But then, there is the most important refocus the U.S. has to make: the total reforming and revitalization of its education system. This must be a national effort with an integration and utilization of local resources. This will mean a national focus on purposes and general direction with important seed funding but with local administration, funding, and management. Parents and teachers will be the key to its success. Projects, such as the "Harlem Children's Project," that focus on each child from primary school through high school, that forms a working relationship between parents, teachers, and the child, will be the central part of the system. The new approach must have a laser focus on bringing our children into the new century so that from positions, as shown in a recent study of 34 leading countries, of 14th in reading, 17th in mathematics, and 27th in science, American children can once again be counted as among the best-educated in the world.

The goals must be for 100 percent graduation from secondary school or a national vocational school system and development of a new generation of well-educated technicians. Apprenticeship programs, such as those used in Germany, that lead to well-qualified and well-paid professional technicians will lead to more productive 21$^{st}$ century technology companies.

With an emphasis on federal austerity, shifts can be made in both emphasis and funding from such questionable expenditures as worldwide wars and massive incarceration, to training and preparing American youth to bring this nation to its potential once again. As an example, imagine the funding available for educating American youth by reducing to one half the 2.3 million persons incarcerated and by cutting in half the expenditures on war making experienced in the last 10 years. Consider how many youth could be trained by utilizing for education the $50,000 spent annually on incarcerating each prisoner in America or how many at risk youth could be saved by diverting the $1,000,000 annually currently spent on each soldier in Afghanistan to teaching American children.

Among the most admired and most productive aspects of American society in the late 20th century was the technological innovativeness that brought such things as the personal computer, satellites, cellular phones that revolutionized communication, websites, search engines, social networking, Facebook, Twitter and Shout It Out, on-line gaming, and so on. Federally funded programs with national focus developed from defense spending and other nationally funded efforts were directly responsible for the internet, for satellite technology, and for the development of the new circuitry and microelectronics that led to such innovations as the cell phone, the iPad, and the e-reader. Our efforts in space have led to countless new products such as high caloric drinks and special high-heat resistant, light-weight fabrics. The Chinese are committing $1.5 trillion to developing green-oriented, new technological manufacturing enterprises. For years, Japan and Europe have focused on high speed rapid transit. The United States must again make it a national priority to invest in such futuristic systems. Without such a new focus on investment, the U.S will become a secondary economic player in the world economy.

If the U.S. moves from a focus of massive incarceration to a more humane and libertarian system, more at-risk youth will be prepared for productive and useful lives. This will have the effect of turning the negativity in the lost generation of inner city youth into a positive force. Such a new emphasis, when combined with a downsizing of the use of U.S. military troops, will result in changing the country onto a more positive trajectory. A shift in the U.S. military focus will have the immediate effect of refocusing the efforts of a major part of America from the destructive to the positive.

Much energy is now being devoted to the question of illegal immigration. Whole industries such as hotel, construction, and large-scale commercial agriculture depend upon these illegal immigrants to do jobs that few Americans are willing to do because of the labor-intensive content and relatively low wages. A page from the German and French solutions to similar situations can be followed. Guest worker visas could be issued to allow the worker to work legally at these hard, low paying jobs. Rather than arresting and deporting these workers, such a shift in immigration policy would accelerate America's economic development. An analysis of American history will show that such waves of European immigration helped fuel the growth of a young America in prior centuries.

America must regulate its financial institutions to control the speculation which led to the bubble that imploded causing the 2008-09 financial meltdown. In this regard, focus must be on transparency of transactions such as derivatives that have been developed and traded by the major banks without regulation. Analysis must look at whether the huge, quasi-public support to housing should be continued. It is easy to say the American dream is for each American to own his or her own home. The harder question is whether it is financially feasible or even desirable, and whether the country is willing to pay for this luxury. Sometimes, Americans are quick to want things without analyzing and understanding the cost. It isn't that the country should stop dreaming and funding projects for the future growth but careful thinking and planning should be done as to cost/benefit.

## *Austerity and Growth*

There is no doubt that there must be adjustments to federal and state budgets both in income and in expenditures. The world will no longer fund America's extravagances, nor should it. The new Tea Party movement has half the equation right. There must be some adjustment in the federal budget to bring down the huge deficit. It is wrong to blame the present deficit on either political party alone. It is a culmination of years of budgetary malaise and lack of foresight and planning.

A series of measures are required from the standpoint of prudent fiscal management. A goal must be to bring the federal deficit down to a manageable 3 percent of GDP or less as tax revenues increase due to an improved economy. There also must be significant cost cutting. While no American politician seems to want to speak of it, increased tax revenue will also be required. A complete restructuring of the existing tax code with the objective of closing tax loopholes would make the system more equitable and could generate up to a trillion dollars in additional tax revenue.

It is possible to reduce the federal budget deficit to manageable level within 5 years. However, probably more importantly, there must be a change in the direction of America to a new posture. This will require the following:

1) A total restructuring of health care. This began with the Obama administration but met with huge resistance. America must realize that, if equitable health care is given to all Americans, it will cost the country. However, either the country faces this or its current chaotic course will lead to even higher health care costs with marginally realizable benefits;

2) A total restructuring of national defense with the goal of closing most bases worldwide and the curtailment of the continuous war cycle the United States has embarked upon in the past 10 years. The goal should be to cut defense spending from 25% to 50 percent in the next 5 years;

3) Some major adjustments in both age and benefits paid by Social Security. While the system is currently liquid, there is no question that its solvency is jeopardized if such adjustments are not made;

4) A total rethinking of the United States' immigration system. The question of immigration should not so much be the xenophobic focus on legality as it should be on the policy of allowing entry of both lower and higher skilled immigrants with permits to fill jobs that Americans will not fill. Some type of guest worker program for low wage farm, hotel, and construction workers must be structured. Additionally, high-tech workers should be sought and stimulated to come to the United States;

5) A total restructuring of the United States criminal justice system. It is simply uneconomical and is a social negative

to incarcerate the number of prisoners for the lengths of time the United States presently does. The goal should be to cut in half the present number of incarcerated persons in the United States. This can be achieved by such measures as changes in mandatory minimum sentences, bringing back a system of parole, rehabilitation through education and retraining, a change in focus of a number of criminal laws, and alternatives to incarceration for non-violent, first-time offenders.

6) A new program of national focus on research and development efforts such as the country has had in the past. Federal funding for such projects, through universities, should be emphasized with the private sector used to bring these projects to the market;

7) A new focus on education. The nation must stop the decay to its primary and secondary school systems. New emphasis on paying teachers better, on bringing the best of America's young professionals into teaching, and on rewarding excellence in teaching must be made. A national program of vocational training and of online, virtual teaching must be instituted. Without these changes, the present educational system in America will not produce the trained people to allow it to reshape itself into the advanced technologically-based economy it must be in this new century;

8) A tightening of the laws and regulations as to the use of financial derivatives by the banks so that the use of these instruments is more transparent. This began with the Obama administration's passage of the Financial Reform Act of 2010 but should be further expanded with exchanges set up to handle the actual listing and sale of such derivatives. Also, banks should have to collateralize such derivatives with sufficient capital (considerably more than the 10 percent in the present bill);

9) A better equalization of income and wealth should be aimed for in the United States through improvements in opportunities for middle and lower classes, not by "robbing the rich." In the past 20 years, the distribution of wealth

and income has become increasingly distorted with the wealthiest Americas growing ever more wealthy and the middle class getting poorer.

10)  A new international currency with the U.S. dollar no longer the hegemonic reserve currency and currency of trade. Either the United States works at developing such a new monetary system in a structured manner or it will be forced into such a new system by the markets. A structured transition would be far better for the economic well-being of the United States.

## Balanced Budget

For the past 30 years, the United States has collected federal taxes which approximated 18 percent of GDP. However, its expenditures have been over 20 percent of GDP. As shown in this book, this has exploded the federal debt and has been financed by other countries and people buying the U.S.' Treasury bonds. Because of the size of the present deficit, if the political will exists, there could be something approaching a balanced budget within the next 5 years. If this is not done, there will be financial catastrophe facing the U.S. as its debt becomes unserviceable.

The United States has the potential to both undertake austerity measures and to work at new reforms to stimulate growth. These will require discipline, some pain, and planning. The United States is of sufficient strength to make such changes and to continue to be a leading economic and political power in this century. The question is whether the United States has the collective wisdom and the political will to change its course and make the necessary structural changes to continue its greatness. A firm, transparent plan will reduce the uncertainty among businesses and citizens, helping to boost economic growth. A failure to make the course change will be disastrous to the United States in the long term.